OWN THE AMERICAN DREAM

**Getting
your castle
without
the hassle**

**How to get
the home
you want**

MIKE DOMER

Own the American Dream

ISBN: 0-929874-99-4

Library of Congress Catalog Card Number: 95-68361

Printed in the United States of America

Cover Design: *Tim Fisher*

Printed by: *McNaughton & Gunn, Inc.*

                      Saline, Michigan 48176

Published by: *Gita Saraydarian*

Note: Mike Domer and Mike Domer Productions are not engaged in the business of providing loans for the purchase and refinancing of homes. Mike Domer and Mike Domer Productions have not made an independent evaluation and/or inspection of any property in question. Mike Domer and Mike Domer Productions make no representation or warranties, implied or expressed, concerning the adequacy, suitability, physical condition or status of any real property, including but not limited to the physical size or attributes of the property, or whether there are any disclosed or undisclosed defects concerning any property. Mike Domer and Mike Domer Productions make no representation regarding the successful implementation of the contents in this book. The success of home buying is totally up to the individual.

This book is intended for guidance only and is not provided as legal advice, investment advice, or advice on any specific or general real estate issues and purchases. The information contained is the opinion of the author based on many years of training and experience in the field of real estate. Neither the publisher nor the editors make any claims to the material contained.

Please consult legal, financial, or any other professional advice for your purchases and real estate and financial decisions.

"Dynamite information. I was reading this book while looking for a home. I couldn't wait to get to the next chapter."

— S.A. Phoenix, AZ

"I've rented a home for two years for $1,200 a month. Now, I have a home, and pay $840 a month mortgage. Thank you for your great help."

— S.S. Cave Creek, AZ

"I did just what you said — got pre-approved for $150,000 and found my dream home."

— J.A. Boston, MA

*"I thought I was so flexible, surely I could find my home. Wrong. **Too** flexible. So, I started making my Dream Lists and visualizing just what I wanted and I found it in two months!"*

— S.E. St. Louis, MI

"Your book is great. Organized. To the point. We love it. It makes buying a home easier."

— Mr. & Mrs. M.J. Los Angeles, CA

"I give this book to all my clients. They get to dream and we help each other find their Dream Home."

— C.F. Los Angeles, CA

"I got a great fixer-upper. I love my new home. Thanks for the help."

— L.T. Chicago, IL

"My home is perfect. I listened to your advise and have a home I can live in for a few years, then re-decorate. More importantly, I have pride in myself."

— H.S. Honolulu, HI

"My self-esteem and self-confidence took a jump. Nothing like owning a home. Thanks."

— S.B. Richmond, VA

"I can use all my artistic talents to decorate my new castle. Thanks for all the tips."

— J.S. Sarasota, FL

"Home shopping was so stressful for my husband and me until we took your advice — now we're enjoying the process and shopping for our Dream Home. Thanks!"

— M.C. Providence, RI

"I thought I could think of everything regarding what my family needed in a home until I read your wish lists — they helped me get very clear and organized and made dealing with my broker easier."

— C.D.T. Plano, TX

"Getting pre-approved put me in control and we were able to negotiate a better deal with the seller."

— E.S. Forest Hills, NY

"After reading your book, I was able to make the right decision for me between a fixed rate mortgage and an ARM."

— M.P. Salt Lake City, UT

"I was paying $940 a month for an apartment. Using your book and working with my lender, the tax benefits I realize allows me to pay $1,160 a month for a home that is mine."

— S.M. Denver, CO

Table of Contents

Acknowledgments

This book originated from four major sources: Constant travel over the last seven years; research; consulting; and personal experiences. My public speaking has put me in contact with all types of people in every part of the United States and Canada. I listened and observed. The people I met had two characteristics in common whether they were real estate agents or home buyers:

1. The mortgage process was too complex and they did not understand it.

2. They didn't know how to get the process to work for them.

I have trained over 300,000 real estate agents and helped them meet their customers' needs. Now, I am turning my attention to you, the home buyer.

I am very fortunate that some terrific and gifted people took a personal interest in me, my work, and this book *Own the American Dream*. I want to acknowledge and thank these people. First, I want to thank my wife, Peggy, who provided me the emotional support and encouragement necessary to complete the book. I am grateful for her support and willingness to allow this project to dominate many of our conversations, and her respect for my personal goals and life's work. She is a source of inspiration.

Elliot Srebrenick, a gifted consultant, contributed his considerable brainpower to the ideas contained in this book. He is a source of marketing brain power and professional candor.

Lou Schwartz, with whom I worked in promoting our real estate classes, provided a rich understanding of you, the home buyer and your needs. He never let me forget your needs.

I also would like to thank Frank Vigarino, whom I affectionately call my "schlepper." Frank carries these books to you and to people all over the United States along with the help of Linda Basso and Laurie West. I thank Debi Merriott, who keeps score for me; Neela Shah my administrator; Barbara Salisbury, who helped type and copy; and my entire team that brings you to my American Dream.

No one writes a book alone. Some of the ideas in this book are mine and some are from other sources long forgotten. I wish to acknowledge the contributions others have made to my life by freely sharing their thoughts. It is my sincere desire that you may benefit from the ideas and thoughts in this book and share them with others. It doesn't matter what you can do... what matters is what you will do!

People think I'm a magician, that I can do magic. They pay me a lot of money to do impossible things and create deals for impossible people under a complex and contradictory real estate system. It's no magic. My mother taught me everybody has to get a piece of the Pie; find a way to help people and they'll help you. Everybody's got to feel good. So I developed a good eye and a clean cut to slice the pie so everyone wins. That has been my legacy.

I'm an agreeable guy. I listen a lot; people feel good because I get them to listen to each other. I play some golf, dream, work hard, never tell dirty jokes, sleep with my own wife, and love the Lord with all my heart. That's all about Mike Domer. That's who I am. Now, let me help you get your piece of the American Dream.

Drop me a line and let me know what your thoughts are on this book and this subject. I like to expand and grow in my service to you, the home buyer, and all your suggestions and comments are welcome.

Mike Domer

1995

Preface

"You are a king by your own fire-side, as much as any monarch in his throne."

— Cervantes, *Don Quixote* (1605)

I believe that you can get your castle without the hassles normally involved in the process of buying your Dream Home.

You can own your part of the American Dream. You have choices, and you should be free to act on them.

Over the last seven years, I have personally trained over 300,000 licensed real estate agents on how to sell homes. During this time, I realized the tremendous need to help buyers buy their dream home. I know that there is so much information on real estate, buying a home, and financing, but I wanted a book that showed you specifically how you can empower yourself and successfully proceed on this very important process of your life. Let's stop being overwhelmed with the choices, decisions, options, and the endless trail of paperwork.

I am here to help you simplify the process. I reveal in this book how you can gain the benefits of being a cash buyer, regardless of your income and amount of down payment.

My focal point is to awaken you to the fact that the mystique of home buying has been distorted. Most of you believe that you first look for a

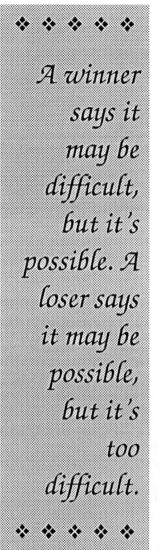

A winner says it may be difficult, but it's possible. A loser says it may be possible, but it's too difficult.

home by yourself, or find an agent who will give you some choices. You look and look until something grabs you. After looking endlessly, you find a home and you begin the process of securing a mortgage. The feeling of insecurity, the endless trail of paperwork, the waiting, and the feeling that maybe you haven't made the right choice haunt you day and night.

This can be an ineffective and frustrating process. It is a myth that has been continuously perpetuated. As it exists today, this process creates inconsistencies, confusion, delay, fear, hassle, and lack of control.

We will show you a different way to buy your home: you get your loan first. Then, you know what price home you can afford, how much down payment you need, and you have bargaining power with the seller to help you negotiate the best deal.

Instead of chasing rainbows with real estate agents and finding out you can't qualify for the homes they are showing you, getting frustrated and tired, you now have the right system.

We will show you how to gain control of your destiny and help you get your dream home faster, and use someone else's money, the lenders'.

Is this too simple and obvious? I have been teaching this **"Reverse Process"** to large numbers of people. I have trained over 300,000 real estate agents in this process. Now, I see the need to pass this information to you, the home buyer.

The process of buying a home should be a joy and easy to complete. Why have so much pain and agony? The purchase of your home, be it the first time or the 10th time, should be an experience of achievement, success, self-esteem, and making a part of your life's dreams come true. This is the American Dream....

To me, the American Dream means to:

— own my own home and property

— have a good job or business

— get ahead

— have security and a stable environment for me and my family

— have fun and psychological well being

— do good for neighbors and community

— be productive and responsible

— have continued success, prosperity and a healthy self-image

These benefits can be attributed to home ownership. Why? Think about it. So many of our ancestors came to America because they knew that there are opportunities here never before dreamed of. People all over the world don't have the ability to own land and homes as we do in America. In the recent past all over the world, the only people who owned homes were the Lords, the landed gentry. They had huge castles and estates and ordinary people worked for the landlords for their entire lifetime. Our ancestors came to America and built a dream that included the right to own property regardless of their social status.

This has not changed much from the early days of America. We all still want this part of the American Dream and will work to keep it. If you work hard and stay focused, you can have success in all parts of your life.

Owning a home is very important to your dreams and financial, emotional, and mental well-being. As you sleep your home is building equity, an asset that you can't have while renting. A home provides security. Home ownership gives you stability. You develop roots in your community.

When we commit to a community, we become more socially responsible. We begin to invest in the community and take care that our investment is well cared for; that the value of our home and our lifestyle does not deteriorate; we care what happens to our community, our children, our homes. We do not want to live in fear. When we have a vested interest, we want to make sure that interest is secure.

Bright futures start in sunny kitchens. When you buy a house, you are building a safe, secure, and a happy home; your just reward, a place to relax and enjoy life.

Homes are affordable and many options exist to get into a home. There are exciting choices. It is a sign of the times.

So, if you want to own your castle without the hassle, start picturing and imagining yourself in your dream home **RIGHT NOW**.

Through these pages, I will show you how you can make part of your dreams come true.

Realize that there are times when you may need additional advice or expertise on a particular aspect of your purchase. Always seek professional advise when you feel in doubt or when you need it. Contact your lender, real estate agent, contractor, lawyer, etc.

This list provides the basics of home buying. We cover the following:

1. Finding a lender

2. Finding the best and most suitable loan

3. Finding a good agent

4. Finding your dream home

5. Negotiating for the best deal

6. Buying your home

7. Charts, references, work sheets

This material is practical, down-to-earth and it works.

Believe in yourself — and enjoy your castle.

Remember, owning a home

— builds financial, emotional, mental security

— provides the roots for the branches of your real happiness, family unity, enhanced self-image

— is a compelling factor to organize your life, your work, your play, your family life

— helps you be creative and healthy as you maintain your home, decorate, garden, and perform general up-keep

— gives you pride of ownership

— gives you opportunity for advancement financially as you build credit and equity in your home

— best of all, it gives you immeasurable joy, sense of accomplishment, and a sense of being in the winning part of society

So much more comes with owning a home. So much is personal and hard to measure.

One thing for sure: we are all here to be part of this American Dream.

Introduction

"The most fortunate of men, be he a king or commoner, is he whose welfare is assured in his own home."

— Goethe (1787)

Why am I writing this book?

It's always been part of everyone's "American Dream" one day to own your own home. Yet as the years go by, more and more Americans are led to believe their dream of owning their own home will never be realized.

My wife Peggy and I felt too cramped in the little apartment we were renting when our son Michael arrived. I was browsing through the classifieds looking for apartments to rent, when my eye caught an ad that read, "Duplex, live in one side and let the other help make your payment. Less than $2,000 down."

I called on the ad and the agent coaxed us into taking a look. He gave us an address and told us to meet him at the property. The young agent arrived at the property 10 minutes late in a brand new Corvette. He was dressed in an expensive, flashy suit. We were already impressed.

The agent was representing his broker who had apparently purchased a development of about 30 duplexes from a nearby hospital. Over the last 15 years, the hospital had been renting the units to resident doctors and nurses. The units had been updated by the new owner who brought them into compliance with the then FHA and VA requirements. They weren't much to look at, but they were freshly painted and clean. Each unit had 2 bedrooms, living room, kitchen, a bathroom, no garage and enough back yard space to keep our son occupied. The price of the duplex was $18,500 and could be moved into with 10% down. Based on the agent's calculations, after renting the other side out, we would only have to come up with an additional $75 per month to make the house payment. That sounded pretty good because that was 1/3 of our current rent.

Like most first time home buyers, we were nervous. We didn't want to make a mistake. We thought it would be a good idea to have my father look at the property before we made any decisions. My dad had been a general contractor of homes and had designed and built dozens for others. Who better to help a first time home buyer make a decision? The agent tried to discourage us from getting my father involved He said he could not guarantee he could hold the duplex we wanted while we tried to get my father to look at it. I told him, since there were still 20 left to pick from, I would take my chances.

My father took a quick look at the property. He wasn't impressed. He said the duplexes were cheaply built and had no basements, which is frowned upon in northeast Ohio. He told us if we should buy one of them, not to ask for his advice again.

Now we had a dilemma: If we buy the duplex, we risk the possibility of alienating my father. If we don't buy, we go back to renting. Our $75 contribution to the mortgage payment looked better than the rent payment, so we bought the property.

After we moved in and were able to find a renter for the other side, we found our monthly contribution to the mortgage payment was closer to $125. Although it was not the $75 a month we had hoped for, it was still lower than paying rent. My dad was right about the construction. As time went on, little repairs became more frequent. We decided to sell the property after 2 years and managed to get $31,500 for it. After deducting real estate commissions and other expenses, we had realized a profit of over $10,000 on our duplex! Our first time buying experience had taught us several things:

1. You can own a home for less than what you can rent.

2. It doesn't take a fortune to buy a home.

3. Getting others involved in the decision making process isn't always the best idea.

4. Sometimes, you can be stupid in real estate and still make money.

Buying our first home did many things in our lives. Other than having children, home ownership gave us a sense of permanence and responsibility. Now that we had a piece of the American Dream, we didn't want to lose it. We became more mature and I worked harder at my job and looked forward to fulfilling another American Dream, a successful career. If we had kept renting we probably would have spent our savings on something that would have depreciated to no value. But our $2,000 investment had grown to $12,000 in two years.

Today, my children are grown and in college. Our needs have changed. In twenty years, our dream home has changed. I am now fulfilling my dream of a million dollar home located on a golf course next to a mountain.

Times change, people change, dreams change.

I have had to work hard to fulfill my dreams. I have had to prioritize my Dream Lists, make compromises and sacrifices, and negotiate hard to reach my dreams. You can do the same....

The purpose of this book is to return this dream to the hearts of Americans. In my book you will learn:

1. The American Dream is alive and well and can be realized much sooner than you think.

2. You can probably own your own home today for less than you are paying in rent.

3. You can own your own home even if you have had credit problems.

4. Owning a home can help your marriage, personal, and business life.

5. Why you shouldn't wait until you can afford the home you want.

6. Why you need to become politically active to protect and preserve the American Dream and safeguard the tax benefits of owning a home.

7. Practical steps in purchasing a home, including:

   a. Why you need to come to terms with your lender before you go looking.

   b. Why using a real estate agent is to your advantage and how to pick the right one.

   c. Why buying the "best" house in a neighborhood is a mistake.

   d. When you buy is how to make money on your home.

   e. How to give yourself tremendous bargaining power over the seller and other buyers.

   f. Why waiting for a down market to buy can be a mistake.

Sometimes I feel lost in the wonder of the world and its gifts. We are so accustomed to doing what others want, doing what's right or doing what we're doing to earn money. We need to go someplace we can call our own, our home, sanctuary, our own castle.

Urban alienation put physical and emotional miles between us, family and friends. Thank God, we can still share quality time with our families and friends. A home is the place we relax, enjoy quality time, a visit, dinner, a meal or other activities. A home gives us the serenity we seek. We still need somewhere to sleep, still need shelter, to be warm, be cool. We need a place to think and do what we want, a place to love, cry, speak, sing, create and even "veg" out.

Man can't live without love. For civilized men and women, love comes with a good home life, roots in the community, a sense of self worth and a sense of accomplishment.

WHEN IS THE BEST TIME TO BUY?

NOW!

I believe you can buy the home of your dreams if you pay attention to the most essential components of buying a home. Some of them are:

1. Be passionate about your priorities. We have a whole set of Passion Lists in this book. If you are not passionate about what you want, you won't get it. Don't be indifferent; feel, act, and think of your dreams.

2. Be prepared to make compromises, and be sure these are things you can live with. You can live without a pool room, but you will need the right number of bathrooms. You **can** change colors, wallpaper, drapes, carpets. You cannot change a noisy street.

3. Prepare your DREAM LISTS and be prepared to negotiate for what you want. You will probably get most of what you have on your DREAM LIST. You can negotiate for anything. The stronger you are in your commitment, the better your chances of negotiating successfully.

4. Visualize just what you want. Build yourself a future where you want to live. Cut out pictures from the Sunday Homes section of your newspaper. (See next page)

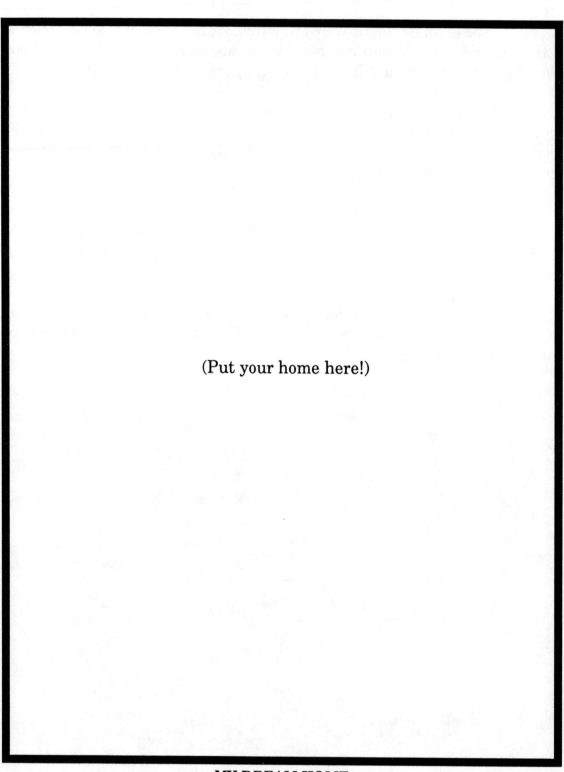

(Put your home here!)

MY DREAM HOME

5. Buy the best house you can afford and work to pay for it. We all have to work. Me...you.... Shoot for buying the least expensive house in the best neighborhood.

6. You are going to get **your** dream home, **your** asset, with other people's money — the lender's. The lender wants to help you. The lender is your partner. If you have any credit problems, clean them up right now. Then take all your information to the lender, and work to get the best loan.

7. Be prepared to sell the lender the idea that you are a good risk — that you will work to get what you want. Have your work and credit history handy. You can use the checklist provided in this book.

I will help you simplify the process as much as possible to help you remove the fears and frustrations in buying a home. I will give you the tools to help you get started.

What you need to do is this:

1. Become a cash buyer by getting a **Pre-approval Commitment Letter** from your lender. I will show you how to do this in a separate section. Your lender is your partner in getting your American Dream so, **get pre-approved**.

2. Decide what is really important to you. Remember you can change most everything about a home. You can put in, take out, anything but you can't change the location. Which brings us to the next point.

3. Decide where you need to live and why. It is really important to be realistic about location. Does your home need to be near schools? Office? Shopping? Entertainment? Public transportation? Medical needs? Do you need a large yard for your pets? A place to garden? Can you spend time and money on a large lawn or upkeep of the yard? Are you going to be away from home a lot? In the back of this book, we have a checklist of the things that you may need to consider regarding location.

4. Decide on what you can afford. How much are you paying now in rent or in mortgage payments? Can you afford to pay more? How much more? figure out your budget. A worksheet is provided for you.

5.   Negotiate with your lender on the type of mortgage that fits your budget. There is a section later in the book devoted to this. Learn as much as you can and be prepared.

6.   Make a Dream List. Besides location, what do you want in a house? What are absolute essentials? What are you willing to compromise? Use the Dream List chart in the back to get you started. Don't be afraid to add and subtract items from the list.

7.   Get a good real estate agent to help you locate the right property. Ask around to your friends and go and talk to them.

8.   Go shopping. Look at everything that may fit your Dream List. Always be alert as to what you can do to fit your dream to your budget.

9.   Negotiate your Dream List with the seller. Remember, everything is negotiable. Know what you want and go into the process well-equipped with this knowledge.

10.   Make your offer and give a deposit to show you are serious with your offer. Be absolutely clear, in writing, of every single thing you are asking the seller to do. If your purchase is based on a list of items that need to be met, list them clearly within your offer. These ten steps will make you a more effective buyer and remove the mystique of your home purchase.

I am going to show you, in more detail in the following pages, how to **REVERSE** the **PROCESS** and get your **castle without the hassle**.

Chapter 1

Get Your Piece Of The American Dream

"It is not enough to aim, you must hit."

— Italian Proverb

If you really want a home, you can have it, but be willing to give what it takes to get it. I believe that there is nothing impossible in this world, given right effort, right timing, stamina, and desire.

Success does not happen by accident. Success is important, but so is being happy and able to enjoy your success.

To achieve success in buying a home, and to be able to have your dream home and enjoy it, you need to set clear priorities. Some people are so set in their ways that making a simple choice is a totally agonizing process. But when you are clear about what you want, and realize what you must do, you will be able to look at many choices and immediately narrow the field.

Face it, making choices and decisions is tough. However, decisions become clear when we address the issues.

This chapter is designed to start you thinking of your priorities in buying a home. If this is your first purchase, then you may not even know what is available. If this is not your first home, then you have some idea of what you want and what you don't want.

This is an important process. Think about your needs and go over your Dream Lists.

HOW DO YOU DEFINE YOUR DREAM HOME?

Let's look at some parameters:

1) Your family size and style — inside spaces

2) Your family size and style — outside spaces

3) Your work

4) Your tolerance level

5) Your Dream Home style

6) Neighborhood

7) Educational, spiritual, & recreational needs

8) Time available for upkeep

9) Funds available per month (this will dictate how flexible you must be with the rest)

Remember — when you are setting your priorities: it is your opinion that really counts. Don't go around asking what people like. They will tell you — and it is strictly *their* opinion of what *they* want. To me, it is futile to get all the opinions of family, friends, etc. It confuses the issue. Also, suddenly, everyone becomes an instant expert:

— Mom knows just what trees to plant where.

— Dad knows just where the tool shed should go.

— Your artist friend is ready to tear the walls down and paint each one a different color.

— Your grandfather says : "just go in, live in it as it is, never mind the carpets, the color, the trees; just save your money!"

— Your sister wants you to throw out all the old furniture and have "large, open spaces" — i.e. empty rooms!

Well, you get the picture. This process is just for you. Don't even tell others about it. Sit down (include spouse and children if possible) and just **Think. Dream. Visualize.**

So, take a piece of paper (or use the chart provided here and in the appendix) and jot down what you need to consider.

We identify ourselves with what we do, rather than what we are. No wonder we feel pressured to do something beyond on a regular basis. In the process of buying a home, we find out who we really are, beyond what others expect of us, beyond what we do, beyond what we earn. We learn what we want and whether it is worth working for.

1. YOUR FAMILY SIZE AND STYLE — INSIDE SPACES

Let's take the items listed one-by-one:

First, consider your family size and style — Are you single? Retired? Just married? Will you have children in the next few years? Do you have a child or children? Do you have a mother/father/etc. who will live with you? Do you have any pets or ones that require special care? Large pets require larger yards. A large dog needs a large yard, etc.

Do you want horses? Then you will need to put that down and make sure your property is zoned for such animals.

Your family style takes into consideration what you do in a normal day or week and weekend. Take a few moments and consider what your typical week looks like. Do you want to maintain this style or do you want a change?

If you now drive one hour to work, do you want to find a home that's closer? Or do you want a home that has an extra bedroom in it for office space? Many homes now have a room or loft that can easily be converted into an office.

Are we engaged in a ruthless, barbarian struggle to increase our comforts, our riches, our lives, our freeway drives? Sometimes we are just like our ancestors choosing to go west to get 40 acres and a mule for a better life and a better future.

Let's go back and consider the following needs:

— Large kitchen and dining area — if you love to cook and entertain casually

— Formal dining room — either for formal dining, or converting to a family/entertainment room

— Total number of bedrooms and bathrooms needed. What kinds and sizes of bedrooms do you most want? Do you want full baths (bathtub & shower); two sinks in the bathrooms, separate shower and toilet? Visualize what you love.

— Do you have hobbies — such as sewing, making crafts, repairing cars and household gadgets, model airplanes? Consider what sort of space you will need for these pleasurable activities.

— Do you exercise? Do you need a gym in your home?

— Consider also the kind of lighting you like. Do you want an open, outdoorsy look, or do you like a soft, cozy home with less windows and doors?

— Consider the area you will live in and the heating and air conditioning needs you have. If you don't know what you want, then start looking at how you use your home/apartment now. Look at your friends' homes. Make a mental note: I like this kitchen; I like this closet space; I want more windows, etc.

Well, you get the idea, just go over whatever family makeup, size, style you have or will have in the near future and fit that reality with what you need to house it.

Think, dream, visualize. Come up with things that are particular and special to you and your family. This is a very important step in being able to enjoy your home when you do finally get it.

Take a look at the attached chart. Fill it out, and if you want, you can take it along when you go house hunting.

Dream List

Your Family Makeup And Inside Livable Space				
ITEM	NUMBER	KIND / SIZE	YES	NO
Number of adults				
Number of children (now or future)				
Number of retired who will live with you				
Pets — cat, dog, birds, other				
Number of bedrooms				
Living room				
Family room				
Home office/library				
Game room, hobby room				
Workout room				
Kitchen — small, medium, large?				
Dining room — formal? informal?				
Bathrooms — half, 3/4, full size				
Windows in bathrooms?				
Basement				
Garage — 1 car, 2 car, 3 car?				
Windows in garage?				
outside door beside garage doors				
attached or detached?				
Heating — heat pump, natural gas, electric, radiant, solar, coal				
Air Conditioning				
Evaporative Cooler				

Chart 1-1 Setting Priorities

Dream List

Other things I want inside my dream home.

What did we accomplish each day in getting our dream? Take a few moments to reflect. Applaud yourself. In fact, take a few hours, hey...take a long weekend...then come back and let's go to the outside of your dream home.

2. YOUR FAMILY SIZE AND STYLE — OUTSIDE SPACES

Next consider the outside of your home and your family size and style.

Yards and properties come in a plethora of sizes, styles, contents. The first thing you need to determine is **what do I want most that I can't do without.**

Do you love to garden? Gardening is one of America's favorite pastimes. Do you love to putter around the house on weekends? Do you prefer no yard or a very small yard that a gardener will take care of? Is your American Dream a TV Guide, your remote control, and a large bag of Doritos?

Look at your weekend and evening schedules carefully. Also, consider the weather, the area, and natural landscaping available. In some of the Southwest homes, at first glance, the yards look barren and scraped. But when you consider the long hot, dry summers and how much it takes to keep a grass lawn green and delicate flowers growing, you will appreciate the no-care yards.

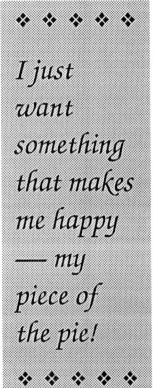

I just want something that makes me happy — my piece of the pie!

A friend of mine bought her first house in Arizona. She promptly cleared the yard, planted flowers, and watered profusely. Summer came. What didn't shrink up and die got eaten by the rabbits! Even if she could, the summer heat prevented any serious gardening or watering. She now has a lovely, low-maintenance desert landscape.

In many neighborhoods around the country, it may be required that you maintain your yard in a way specified by local ordinance or a Homeowners' Association. If you like to garden and maintain a yard, or if you can afford a gardener, then take this into consideration.

Next, consider your outdoor activities. Do you want a swimming pool? A basketball court? A patio for outside barbecues and entertainment? If you spend a lot of time outdoors in your yard, consider the noise level, neighbors, proximity to busy streets, etc.

If you are primarily an indoor person, then many of the outdoor extras are not a priority for you.

Also, do you want a fenced backyard for your children and pets? If the home you like does not have a fence, you will have to add it on yourself.

This may sound like a lot of work but it is not. Be very clear and honest with yourself. Stay with what you want and love most in a yard. Also, be honest about who will care for the yard. Will you do it? Will it be a shared responsibility? Or, will you hire a pool service and gardening service?

Use the chart attached to visualize your dream home. Complete the parts indicated and add anything that you think is very important to you. When setting priorities, it is imperative that you determine what is most important to you and your family. Later, when we consider compromises, you will think of what you must have versus what you can do without.

Begin the process of self-discovery: searching for a home. We have learned to break the intergenerational chain of work ethic. We can decide to be different. We can have dessert before dinner. We have choices....

Be flexible, when we stop looking, stop asking new questions, we lose touch. Things are not necessarily better because we mentally stopped. Are we just tired? Our energy is wasted trying to super-glue today. It is time to stop. HELLO! Take today off...take the weekend off. The moment of personal crises needs some fun, some humor....

Dream List

Your Family Size & Style/Outside Spaces			
ITEM	**KIND / SIZE**	**YES**	**NO**
What kind of garden space do I want?			
What kind of front yard do I want?			
What kind of back yard do I want?			
Do I want a swimming pool?			
Barbecue			
Patio — covered or enclosed?			
Fenced yard			
Total privacy			
Other			

Chart 1-2 Setting Priorities

What other front and back yard qualities do I most want?

3. YOUR WORK

In setting your priorities, your work is an essential component.
Consider the following:

— How far do you drive to work? This will provide you with what you need regarding distance.

— Do I need public transportation? This helps you determine your total commute time. Do you drive and then take public transport? Does this appeal to you? Can you do this?

— If you work at home, what sort of office space do you need? You can convert a bedroom. You can re-model the garage and use a side entrance. You can add on or you may need a home with a separate guest-house for your office.

If you work at home, as so many Americans do now, look closely at what you will need in terms of telephone, outside areas, quiet from family activities, etc.

4. YOUR TOLERANCE LEVEL

I put this here because I know so many people who are not at all bothered by screaming children, barking dogs, lawn-mowers and leaf blowers, outside pool activity, traffic noise, neighbors' loud music and parties, and more.

Others I know cannot tolerate a number of "people or street noises" and really need a more quiet, serene home environment.

This category also fits in with the type of activities you enjoy. If you need quiet, then put this on your priority list. If you have an active family life, then a quiet neighborhood is not a priority for you.

A friend of mine is an active, energetic person. But by nighttime, he likes to read quietly, play soft music, think and be with a few friends. He absolutely cannot live in a noisy, traffic-filled neighborhood. Whereas another family I know just love the hustle-bustle of the family neighborhood they live in. They have no children, yet enjoy the activities of the neighborhood kids.

5. YOUR DREAM HOME STYLE

This deals with the style, size, the construction of your home.

I can't even begin to list all the styles of houses available. The best bet is to get out and drive around and see what you like. Look at the Sunday Home section of your newspaper. There are lots of pictures, ideas, articles that will help you. Subscribe to a home magazine and start putting ideas together. Look in the neighborhoods that are of most interest to you.

The point here is this: if there is a particular look, style, design that is your Dream House, then it is a priority. If you like all kinds of styles, and it really depends on other factors, then style is not your priority but what you can afford is a priority.

Size is also personal. 2,000 square feet of living space is too big for some, too little for others.

Size is important because it is going to affect purchase price and maintenance ease. So, dream, but also be realistic.

6. NEIGHBORHOOD

We touched on this in several places. Remember, the number one rule of real estate is location, location, location. My recommendation is to buy the least expensive home in the best neighborhood you can afford. No matter how beautiful your dream home, if it is in the wrong neighborhood for you, its value is reduced. Or, if it is in a bad neighborhood, overlooking a garbage dump, near a junk yard or a high crime area, soon those charming qualities that you love so much will slowly disappear. However, we have to buy what we can afford. That is a **REALITY,** the "real word."

The location of your dream home determines the price you will pay and later, the resale value it will have. The location will also determine the types of loans, or special government financing available with low interest insured loans.

If the location and neighborhood is still in the planning stage, note just what your priorities are. Get some exercise. Take a deep breath. If you make a mistake, you can always refinance. But, it is hard to move a house. Remember: location, location. Buy the least expensive home in the best neighborhood you can afford.

Look at the following list, then use the chart provided to fill in what you most need, or see as a top priority:

1. The condition of the neighbors' homes

2. What the neighbors act like toward strangers

3. How far are

    - grocery stores

    - specialty stores

    - schools

    - libraries

    - clothing stores

    - parks and recreational facilities

    - my neighbors

    - medical care

    - emergency care (police, fire, etc.)

4. Kinds of utilities available (electric, gas, water, septic or sewer)

5. Enforced Homeowners Association rules & regulations (or not)

6. Kinds of restrictions regarding yard, add-ons, parking vehicles, home-based business or office, outside paint and decoration. Do you like to be free and creative? Or, do you want a more conventional, manicured environment and enforced regulations regarding your yard and home, like a Town House or Condominium?

Mark off where your priorities are regarding neighborhood on the dream list on the next page.

Dream List

Neighborhood			
ITEM	TOP PRIORITY	MED. PRIORITY	NO PRIORITY
Condition of other houses			
Friendliness of neighbors			
Good schools			
Strict Homeowners' Association Rules			
Proximity of:			
grocery store			
specialty foods			
schools			
libraries			
colleges			
clothing stores			
parks & recreational facilities			
my neighbors			
medical care			
emergency care			
gas lines			
high power electric lines			
radio towers			
sewer hook-ups			

Chart 1-3 Setting Priorities

Dream List

What other items in a neighborhood are most important to you?

I would like you to consider also your individual and family's continued educational needs. Whether you are going to finish your academic degree, or volunteer part-time in teaching, consider how far these institutions are, or do they exist at all in your community.

7. EDUCATIONAL, SPIRITUAL, AND RECREATIONAL NEEDS

Look at your spiritual needs, look for places of worship that are within a reasonable distance from your home. If you need spiritual upliftment from non-conventional places of worship, and this is an important part of your life, then add this to your priority list.

Recreation is also a factor to consider. Do you watch home videos? Go out to dinner? Theater? Do you need to be near museums and other cultural places? What about entertainment and after school activities for your children?

Consider also health spas and gyms. If you work out several times per week, it is nice to have a YMCA nearby, or other public or private facilities.

Consider all your recreational needs and make a list.

8. TIME AVAILABLE FOR UPKEEP

What kind of spare time do you have for repair and maintenance of your Dream Home? Your honest answer to this question will determine the size of home you set your heart on, type of yard, condition of your home when you first purchase it.

This is the modern, human experience. We do two things at once. We lead busy lives, become distracted from the process of life. Go with the flow — relax — feel the fullness of life and go on.

Are you good with fixing the washer in the leaking kitchen faucet or do you scratch the porcelain and break your left index finger like I do? Make some provisions in your home agreement for the seller or agent to provide a home service policy.

Existing homes may already be remodeled and in a clean, well-kept condition. Or, if you are handy, you can get a real fixer-upper and turn it into your Dream Home. A friend I have bought a very small home on a 2 1/2 acre lot. The home needed totally new plumbing, electrical wiring, floors, roof, heating and air conditioning, new appliances and new tile, plus inside wall repair. But, she is so handy and loves the challenge of creating her Dream Home that she bought the small house and worked hard to repair it.

Also, you may want a newly built house so everything is modern and clean.

Whatever you want, always consider how much time, skills, and money you have for maintenance and repairs. If you have never owned your own home, then typically any repairs were done by the landlord. Now, **you** are the landlord.

9. FUNDS AVAILABLE PER MONTH

On your priorities list, put down what you now pay in monthly rent or mortgages. Now, how much more can you afford to pay? Do you need to work extra hours or will your family income be able to handle additional expenses? We will go over this in detail in the next chapter.

So, here you are, nine points to consider when setting your priorities for your Dream Home.

Remember, get pre-approval first and get your pre-approval letter to become a cash buyer. Then set your priorities.

Why set priorities? Because when you go out shopping for a home, you will be less frustrated, more educated, have a well thought-out plan and be able to work more effectively with your real estate agent. Finding a home should not be a traumatic experience. It should be fun and full of anticipation.

Also, when you set your priorities, you will be surprised to see how lesser ones will be easily compromised. It is truly an educational process.

So, use the charts in this chapter and in the appendix to determine just where your priorities lie.

Chapter 2

How Much Money Do I Need To Buy A Home?

"With money in your pocket, you are wise and you are handsome and you sing well too."

— A Yiddish Proverb

Across the United States, ever rising home prices has failed to deter first-time home buyers. Nationally, first-time buyers accounted for 47% of all home sales in 1994. This has been the case despite rising interest rates.

Nationally, home buyers faced the challenge of higher loan rates, higher home prices, while their median income dropped by 3.2%. Single family homes accounted for the highest percentage of sales, while condominium purchases came in second.

This means that no matter what happens in the nation, people still buy homes. The market goes up or down, and we all still dream about owning a piece of land, a piece of the pie.

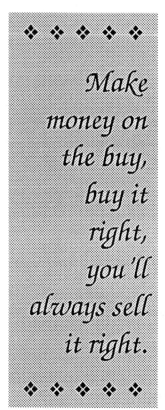

Make money on the buy, buy it right, you'll always sell it right.

If you are one of millions of Americans who wants a place to call home, then buying your own home is what you need to concentrate on. Why throw money away by renting?

We end up slaves to our definition of success. Pigeons live off other people's crumbs and have no need to acquire their own. Human beings need to acquire their own property. What's our goal? Don't develop tunnel vision. We become obsessed with our waist line, the mid-line, the finish line. The real reward is to remove all lines and just concentrate on the bottom line. What do **you** want?

Can you make money on a home? The best time to make money on your property is when you buy. If you buy right, the dollar spread is the profit when you sell. Profit is measured by time and money.

If you have $10,000 to invest, what would bring you the best results?

If you put that into a CD at 5.5% interest compounded over 5 years, you will have $13,070. You have made an average of $614 per year.

If you use the $10,000 as a down payment in a $100,000 home, and your home appreciates 5% per year, your home is worth a total of $127,628 at the end of 5 years. If you take out the cost of sale of your home — 7% is $8,934 — you have $118,694. Subtract the $100,000 cost of the home and you have netted $18,694 in 5 years. This is $3,739 per year, or an average of 37.4% return on your investment. We are assuming here that your mortgage payments and your rental payments, or previous home payments are the same.

If you plan to stay in your home a long time, chances are you will not lose on your investment. The market will go up, you will have made a good choice, and you had years of wonderful living. You have also improved your lifestyle!

Let's go now to the question of how much money do you need to buy a home. Remember that what you now pay in rent and your tax savings on home ownership can give you a bigger and better lifestyle.

A friend of mine recently told me, "I want to know how much I have and what I can spend. I don't want others to dictate what my budget should be."

I have a surprise for you. You should always set your own budget "comfort zone." But, your lender **will** tell you how much you can afford and how much loan you can get. You may get even more than you figured!

Most lenders today have non-qualifying loans. If you put down 25%, you do not have to qualify or have income verified. You still need good credit.

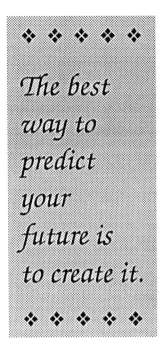

The best way to predict your future is to create it.

Before you go looking for a home, before you talk to your lender, you must have a clear picture of what kind of income you have and what are your expenses. You need to know what you pay for rent or monthly mortgage, utilities, repair bills. Also, what if any non-anticipated expenses come up, how are you prepared to handle them. Do you have children soon to be going to college? Do you have large credit card debts? Do you have good insurance?

Taking a look at your finances gives you a clear idea of what you can afford. Remember, you want the most home for your money. Also, the price of home is not as important as how much you can afford to pay. The price is too high if you can't afford it.

Finding a solid home in a good neighborhood may be better than trying to bag a bargain. Your property values are more likely to go up in a better home and better neighborhood.

Also, having all your financial records, knowing your budget and potentials is important because all lenders will take a close look at your financial situation.

Here are the main areas you need to calculate:

Gross Salary: Total your monthly and annual income before taxes. Do this for yourself and co-purchaser (spouse, family, etc.). Add all your income: savings, salary, and whatever income you have that is a **regular** part of your salary.

Typically, a lender requires two years worth of records, such as copies of your income tax papers. Whatever income you have reported on your tax form is taken into account. Unreported income does not count. If you are self-employed, be sure you have good records.

Lenders want to see what is your **average income**. They want to make sure you have been steadily employed or now have steady income. Two years of steady employment is usually a good indicator but sometimes less is also a positive indicator. A new job may even get you a mortgage. It all depends on your ability to sell the lender that you are a good risk.

Most lenders will consider verifiable income. So, if you receive bonuses, child support, alimony, you can include them. However, your employer may need to write a letter regarding the bonus — that is

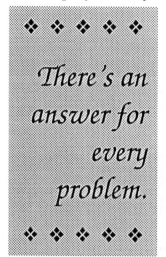

There's an answer for every problem.

dependable income paid on a regular basis. You may also need copies of your legal settlement statements that state the amount you are entitled to receive on a monthly basis. Use the following table to calculate your annual income.

If you are getting a cash gift from relatives, plan early to get it and deposit into your account. This reduces the lender's anxiety about your source of funds and simplifies your application process.

Did you know that up to one-half of first-time home buyers in Florida use cash gifts as part of their down payment?

Federal gift tax rules allow you to receive up to $10,000 per year without having to pay tax. In addition, two parents can each give up to $10,000 per year to their child — a total of $20,000 for a down payment without creating tax liability

If you plan to use a cash gift, you will need to document the source of the gift. You need a "gift letter" from the donor stating the amount received and that it is **a gift not a loan.** The lender may need a bank statement showing that the donor has sufficient funds to give the money — typically to show it is not a cash advance on a credit card.

How much of your gift money you can use for down payments is governed by lending rules. The FHA rules state that a gift can cover the entire down payment, closing costs, and prepaid items. FHA only limits the amount of money you can borrow.

VA loans are available to qualified veterans with no down payment. There are however, related costs, such as closing costs, loan interest points, prepaid items, that can be covered by a cash gift.

Conventional loans may require that 5% of the purchase price be your own money if the loan is greater than 80%. If the gift is 20% of the purchase price, you do not need your own money. At this threshold, private mortgage insurance is not required, so you can save $35-$40 on a $120,000 loan.

So, if you are getting a cash gift, try to get it as soon as you can and put it in your bank.

Use the chart "Personal Asset Data" in this chapter to calculate your assets.

Now you are ready to calculate your expenses. What concerns lenders are your long-term debts. There are debts that will need ten months or more to pay off. For some loans (VA or FHA — more on these later) your monthly utility expenses and other monthly expenses are taken into consideration.

Collect all your monthly payments and total them: car loans, student loans, credit card payments, insurance payments (auto, medical), alimony and child support, payments on any other loan, and so on. Use the worksheet at the end of the chapter to calculate your monthly debts.

If your outflow exceeds your inflow, your upkeep will be your downfall.

What we are getting at is this: What are you paying now for your rent or monthly mortgage? This is the least amount that you can pay and stay in the lifestyle you are in now. These rules apply if this is going to be your first home or your 6th. Next you must figure your insurance, taxes, and the cost of a new Homeowner's Insurance policy (which insures appliances, heating, AC, etc.). Also, figure utilities if you do not pay for them now.

Next, go over your personal assets that you can translate into cash. Use the chart below to calculate what you have. Your assets can be used toward your down payment, closing costs, prepaid costs, and any remodeling you want to do — even moving expenses. Sometimes you can include the cost of remodeling and appliances in your mortgage if you don't have extra cash.

If you want to put together a detailed budget, list every expense including clothing, food, gas, entertainment, then do this for your own peace of mind. I recommend doing this because then you can see areas where you can cut down and have additional money for a larger monthly payment. This translates into a more expensive home for you.

You can try to estimate your mortgage yourself based on financial charts available from bankers, agents, mortgage companies. However, I feel it is best to be armed with your income and expense figures, then go to a qualified loan officer or agent, and figure out your estimated mortgage based on what the market is doing right now. That way, you are working with contemporary home prices and interest rates.

When faced with the consequences of your actions or inactions, you can hold on to the pain, the shame, the blame or move on and use the magic words — "I'm sorry....But I gotta get a home, some place to live, some place that's mine."

Once you have all your income and expenses figured out, you can apply for pre-approval for a loan.

Let's talk about getting **Pre-approval** and becoming a cash buyer in our next chapter.

Dream List

ITEM	YOU	SPOUSE/PARTNER
Gross Salary		
Bonuses, commission		
Interest Income		
Dividends		
Social Security		
Pension funds		
Alimony		
Child Support		
Other		
Total (each column)		
Grand Total (both columns)		

Chart 2-1 Your Total Income

Dream List

ITEM	YOU	SPOUSE/PARTNER
Car Payment		
Personal Loan Payment		
Student Loans		
Credit Cards Total Payments		
Insurance — auto		
Insurance — life		
Insurance — medical		
Property Payments		
Other		
Total (each column)		
Grand Total (both columns)		

Chart 2-2   Your Monthly Expenses

Dream List

Name		As of	
Description	**Market Value**	**Financing**	**Cash Value**
Cash on Hand			
Checking Account			
Savings Account			
Certificate of Deposit			
U.S. Government Bonds			
Corporate/Other Bonds			
Investment in Business			
Partnership			
Cash Value Life Insurance			
Cash Value Retirement			
Cash Value Profit Sharing			
IRA			
Trust Fund			
Personal Loans Owed You			
Automobile(s) Value			
Recreational Vehicle			
Jewelry			
Collections			
Art			
Furniture			
Appliances			
Computers			
Cash			
Other Assets			
Total Cash Value			
Total Available Cash			
Total Cash Gifts			
Borrowed Money (conventional loans)			
Borrowed Money (relatives)			
Total Cash Available			

Chart 2-3 Personal Asset Data Sheet

Chapter 3

What is a Pre-Approved Loan?

"Where Thou art — that is Home."

— Emily Dickinson, 1836.

Picture this scenario. You spend months searching for the right home with your real estate agent. Finally you locate it, one of the best values on the market. Your agent gets your offer accepted over two others. You go to the lender to apply for your loan. Three days later the lender tells you that he can't loan you the money because of a bad report on your credit. You look at the bad report and you see that it is in error. However, because of lending restrictions, the lender cannot approve a loan until the credit is cleared. Do you know how long it takes to get just a mistake cleared off a credit report? It takes weeks, sometimes months. However, the seller, with two other buyers waiting in the wings, isn't willing to wait until you get your credit problems straightened out, cancels your contract and sells the home to one of the other buyers. You spend three months to find the home of your dreams only to lose to another buyer because of a mistake on a credit report. Sound frightening? It happens all the time.

Or, under the same scenario, the lender tells you they can't loan the money you want based on your income. He says you will have to find a home for $15,000 less. Do you know how hard it is to find a home for $15,000 less when you already have your heart set on the one home?

Every real estate agent can tell you dozens of horror stories similar to this. The buyers end up frustrated and angry at the lender, at the agent, and at the whole home-buying process. **The biggest mistake buyers make is that they look for a home before they get a loan.**

You can't afford to make a mistake like this. This is why I recommend that you take the reverse approach: **GET YOUR LOAN BEFORE YOU START LOOKING FOR YOUR HOME.**

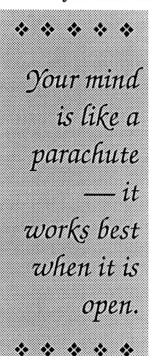

Your mind is like a parachute — it works best when it is open.

When most people finally decide to invest in a home, they can't wait to go out looking. Granted there is nothing better than looking at some nice properties to get you into the excitement of the home buying process, but what is the sense of getting all excited just to have your bubble burst later? Finding a home is not the most important step in securing your piece of the American Dream; it is securing your financing. Unless you have all cash, you can't get a home without the loan.

You might be thinking, why not just get a copy of my credit report? This is not enough. Lenders do not just look at a credit report to determine if they are going to fund a loan. There are many other factors they must consider. No book, computer software, real estate agent, or credit counselor can determine how much you should get and whether you can get a loan. Only the lender can approve you for a loan.

Lenders scare most buyers, but let me tell you, the lender can be your best friend and greatest ally in securing your piece of the American Dream. They don't loan money for the gratuitous benefit of society; they actually make money when they loan money. They want to give you a loan as much as you want to secure one.

Don't be afraid to see your lender right now. He will review your financial situation. He will let you know exactly how much you can borrow. He will show you a variety of loan options. He will discuss the advantages and disadvantages of each. He will check out your credit. If there is a mistake or problem, don't fret. He will direct you so you can get everything straightened out.

How do you determine what lender to go to? Most buyers think that there is some advantage in going to the bank where they have their checking account. In most cases this is not a good choice. Commercial banks specialize in auto loans, credit cards, installment loans, and business banking. In most instances, home loans are not their specialty. You want a lender who offers a variety of programs, one who specializes in retail residential lending. A good real estate agent can direct you to the right lender.

You must insist on a lender who will **pre-approve** rather than pre-qualify you. If an agent says the words "pre-qualify," you may not have the right agent. Pre-qualifying could be a waste of time. To pre-qualify is typically to make an educated guess as to what you may be able to borrow. A lender will run an "in-file" credit report on you. The problem with this is that the "in-file" credit report does not always reveal the entire credit history. The lender will review this along with other information you give him and give you an estimate as to what they might be able to lend you and the price home you can buy. However, this is only an estimate based on the loan officer's evaluation. When you find the home and make a formal application you might be surprised that everything could change.

In order to get a **pre-approved** loan you need to make a formal application. The lender does a full credit report. Your application goes to the lender's underwriting department. Your income is verified. When they are finished, you get a loan commitment for the maximum amount you can qualify. You now have the loan subject to the property appraisal and your credit remaining the same. Now you can go out looking with confidence knowing that when you find your dream home nothing is standing in the way.

If you follow the guidelines outlined in this book, you will be able to pick your Dream Home that is also within your budget.

Typically, a **pre-approved** loan commitment is good for ninety days. However, if you do not locate your home within that period, most lenders will extend your loan for another ninety days with a simple credit update.

Most lenders charge a fee for processing the loan. This is because a full-blown credit report, the paperwork, and the time- spent on the application is time consuming. The usual charge is $50 to $100. This is truly a small price to pay for a peace of mind. You would still have to pay this fee at a later date when you make a loan application. If your lender does not charge for the application, make sure you are getting a **pre-approval letter of commitment.**

There are tremendous advantages in securing a **pre-approved** loan beyond merely knowing where you stand. **Such a loan makes you a cash buyer.** You now have an advantage over other buyers. You won't have to make an offer on a property that is subject to financing. The purchase of the home is not contingent on financing. When a seller looks at an offer that is contingent on financing, he doesn't really know whether his property is sold or not until the financing takes place. In most cases this could take thirty days or longer. However, when he reviews your agreement he will see that you are ready to close the deal.

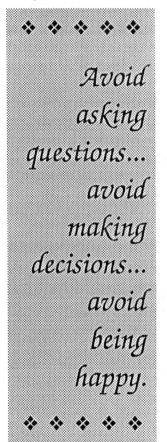

Avoid asking questions... avoid making decisions... avoid being happy.

Without the **pre-approval,** the seller has to wait to see if a buyer can get financed before he knows he has a sale. It is not easy to negotiate a good price when you can't say for sure you can get a loan. But, when you are **pre-approved,** you have the loan. If the seller accepts your offer, he knows his home is sold. If he turns your offer down or tries to negotiate, he knows he risks losing you and the sale of his property. Accepting an offer that is contingent on financing is like accepting something that may never happen. If the seller turns you down, it is like buying his house from you at the price you offer. **Many sellers will accept an offer for less money knowing that you already have your loan rather than take a chance with someone who may never get a loan.** Your pre-approved loan could be worth thousands of dollars to you.

In writing your purchase agreement, rather than stating "subject to financing," you could be so bold as to write, "cash at closing." This will always get the seller's attention! Or, you could state "buyer has already been approved for loan with (name of lender) subject to property meeting appraisal." It is a good idea to give a copy of your pre-approval letter or certificate to the seller when your offer is presented for verification.

Another advantage to having a **pre-approved** loan is that you can close your transaction quicker, typically within a week. Remember a true **pre-approved** means you already have the loan. The only thing that stands in the way is to find the property, appraise the property, complete the title work and close. Most lenders can get an appraisal within a week. The title work and closing documents can be completed within the same period. Once the appraisal is finished, you can close. As I said earlier, most closings take six weeks or longer. You will be able to close your transaction thirty days faster. Not only will this get you into your dream home quicker, but it gives you another advantage in negotiating your transaction.

In states where attorneys traditionally handle closings you could have a problem. Even though you have been **pre-approved** they typically take much longer than lenders or title companies to close transaction. This is the nature of the business. However, like any other business there is always someone out there who wants the business bad enough to get the job done in the time frame you would like. You are going to have to find the firm that can close your transaction quickly in order to take full advantage of the **pre-approval** process. Your real estate agent should be able to help you with this one. Remember, the quicker your transaction closes, the quicker he gets paid too.

Some sellers have already purchased another home. They may have transferred out of town. They could be making two house payments. If you can close thirty days or so quicker, you save the seller a house payment. This could amount to several thousand dollars. You could put this money in your pocket by negotiating a lower price in return for closing quicker on the transaction. A seller who is in financial problems or making two house payments will be prone to take a lower offer knowing that the financial pressure will be gone in a week. Even if the seller does not wish to move so quickly, it is in his advantage to close as soon as possible and know that his property is sold. A rental arrangement can be worked out for a short period to allow him time to get into another home.

I have seen closings being delayed to allow a seller time to find another property. Sometimes when a seller looks in the market place he determines that selling his home at the price and terms he agreed to with you wasn't such a good idea. Now you may have a seller who wants out of the agreement and refuses to close. You might have to hire an attorney to force the closing. This costs you money and no-one wins (but the attorneys) in this situation. It is in your best interest to close on your home as soon as possible. It is also in the seller's best interest as well. The longer the closing is delayed the greater chance the buyer could change his mind as well. No seller wants to enter into a contract on a replacement property only to have a buyer back out on his. It is in everyone's best interest to close as soon as possible. This relieves the anxieties and uncertainties of both parties.

Any intelligent seller will accept your offer over others and at a lower price knowing that you have the loan and can close quicker. Getting a **pre-approved** loan is the most important step you can take in the home buying process. Let me review the advantages.

ADVANTAGES TO SECURING A PRE-APPROVED LOAN COMMITMENT

1. You know what price home you can afford before you start looking.

2. If you have credit errors or problems you can have them corrected while you are looking.

3. In the eyes of the seller, you become a cash buyer.

4. A seller will accept your offer over others knowing you already have your financing arranged.

5. A seller could accept a lower offer over other higher offers knowing that you are a sure thing rather than taking a chance on another buyer, even at a higher price who may never get a loan.

6. You can close within a week and be in your Dream Home.

7. The seller may accept a lower offer knowing you can close quicker and save him money on his house payments.

8. You eliminate the anxiety of buying a home. You know when you find the home you want within the price range you have been approved for, you've got the home.

Chapter 4

Find Your Lender, Get Pre-approval, Become A Cash Buyer$$

"To learn the value of money, it is not necessary to know the nice things it can get for you, you have to have experienced the trouble getting it."

— Philippe Heriat (1946)

Now we will discuss what you need to do to get **pre-approval.** Here is a list of things you will need to consider:

1. Types of lenders

2. Finding a lender

3. Types of loans and financing

4. A clean credit report

The best way to buy your Dream Home is to get a letter of commitment from your lender first. This, in essence, is cash. You become a **cash buyer** when you are **pre-approved and have your pre-approval letter.** This tells your agent and the seller that you can buy this price home NOW!

You have already worked out your monthly income and your monthly expenses as shown in Chapter Two, so you know by subtracting your monthly expenses from your monthly income what you are left with.

Take all your financial information (tax receipts, bank statements, credit card bills, legal agreements, letters, etc.) to your lender. You will now make a written application for a loan. You will be charged for this process. Inquire with your lender about application fees and see if you can negotiate their paying for the loan application.

PRE-APPROVAL OF YOUR LOAN

If you have provided as much complete and accurate information as you can, within a few days (depending on the lender's requirements) you should have an estimate of the loan amount for which you can qualify.

Your lender will check all your records. He will also check your credit record. You can obtain a credit report prior to going to the lender and be ready to answer any questions that may arise.

Write to one of the credit bureaus listed in the Appendix (TRW, TransUnion, Equifax). Include your full name, date of birth, social security number and your present and immediate past address(es). Call them first to determine what you need to send them, such as a fee (sometimes a small fee of $10-$15 will be required) or a copy of your drivers' license or birth certificate.

If you get your credit reports a few months in advance of your loan application, you can correct any unforeseen problems.

If you find errors in your credit report, correct them as soon as possible. Keep a record of all your correspondences.

If you have an outstanding debt, resolve it immediately by writing to your creditor. Send letters explaining the situation to the credit bureau. Make sure your creditor reports changes and resolutions to the credit bureau immediately. Get help if you need it.

If you have had slow payments, this will also appear on your credit report. Send letters to the credit bureau to explain the reasons for late payments and demand they place these letters in your file. Take copies of your letters to your lender.

Clearing bad records and errors takes time. Start this process of checking your credit history as soon as possible when you are ready to get **pre-approval.**

Pay off outstanding credit card charges as soon as you can.

Let me assure you that many people have experienced financial difficulty at one time or another. If you had a difficult time but worked to resolve the situation, you may find that by explaining your experiences honestly and without shame to your lender it will help them help you. Lenders see all kind of financial histories and are there to help you, not embarrass you. The worst that can happen is that you will need to repair some things before proceeding with the loan process but you will then know the steps that will need to be taken to be **pre-approved.**

TYPES OF LENDERS

You are a customer bringing business to a lender. You can select a lender who gives you the best deal and the best service.

There are many kinds of lenders.

1. **Commercial Banks.** Banks sometimes give loans for residential real estate. Check with your local bank.

2. **Mortgage Brokers.** A mortgage broker processes your loan application and submits it to a lender. The lender will then approve the loan.

3. **Mortgage Bankers.** A mortgage banker both processes and approves and services the loan.

4. **Builders & Developers.** Some builders and developers provide loans, making it easy to sell and finance a home.

5. **Government Backed Loans.** FHA (Federal housing Administration) and VA (Veteran's Administration) don't actually

give you a loan. They back home loans, or insure loans. The lender still makes the loan.

6. **Broker-Lender firms.** This is the newest kind of firm that combines buying and financing. These firms offer computerized systems in realty offices that have "financial service" representatives.

7. **Savings and Loan Associations**. They are in the business of lending money for home purchases.

Pre-approval service is beneficial to you. You can find a lender and the system that will give you a quick look at your eligibility in the marketplace. You may have to pay a little more, work a little harder. Today if you want a mortgage, you should be able to find a lender for your needs.

The lender can also offer information on FHA, VA, adjustable rates, low documentation financing for the self-employed, and information for buyers with credit problems.

You will be able to get on customer service ratings, instantaneous scenarios on various mortgages.

You will need to look around and see just what is available for you to get the best deal.

HOW TO FIND THE RIGHT LENDER

You can find a lender by asking friends and relatives. Talk to your friends and find out what sorts of experiences they had with lenders. You need to find one that fits your needs and personal preferences.

Some lenders approach the whole issue of loan application with negativity and a superior, "can't do" attitude. Forget them. You don't need them.

There are good, positive, friendly lenders who are willing to work with you and help you get **pre-approved.** Stay with reputable, friendly, and positive lenders.

Lenders advertise their rates and other loan information. Call and interview them.

Local banks, savings and loans, credit unions, are also good sources if they offer residential real estate loans.

Your real estate agent also can recommend a lender.

See chart 4-1 for some questions you need to ask a lender.

Dream List

QUESTIONS TO ASK YOUR LENDER

1. What types of loans are offered?

2. What is the current interest rate?

3. How many points do you charge?

4. What are the application fees?

5. Do I need mortgage insurance?

6. Can you lock in the rates?

7. Can a loan be prepaid without penalty?

8. What are the escrow requirements?

9. What is the fee for late payment?

10. Do I have a personal contact when I have questions?

11. Who will be my contact person?

Remember: Keep calling your contact person to push for your **Pre-Approval letter.** Find out if they need more information or additional questions answered.

Chart 4-1 Lender Questions

TYPES OF LOANS

There are several types of loans. Some lenders combine several mortgages into a package and sell it to a secondary market. This can be a group of investors who invest in mortgages. If your lender plans to sell your loan, they will let you know. It will not make a difference to you in terms of payments and schedules. However, you need to know that with such lenders, you will need to qualify for loans according to the guidelines set by the loan buyers.

Purchasers can be private companies or government agencies such as Fannie Mae (Federal National Mortgage Association). Freddie Mac (Federal Home Loan Mortgage Corporation), or Ginnie Mae (Government National Mortgage Association).

If you need to find a different type of lender, one without the limits set by the government agencies for example, you will need to get a lender that offers such loans. These types of loans are not structured to be sold to a secondary market. Therefore, they need not meet the requirements of that market.

There are several basic types of home mortgage loans. Loans last as long as it takes to pay the amount of the loan plus the interest. Typically, loans are arranged for 15 and 30 years. Try to get a loan you can pre-pay without penalties.

Winning is the result of good judgment. Good judgment is the result of experience.

Conventional Loans

Conventional home loans are a direct agreement with a lending institution. No government agency is involved.

These loans have either a fixed rate or variable rate of interest. The fixed rate is constant throughout the life of the loan. The variable rate loans, also known as adjustable rate mortgage (ARM), has an interest rate that fluctuates according to economic conditions. The indicator chosen to show the interest rate and increase caps depends on the policy of the lending institution.

The first kind of conventional loan is a **Loan with a Fixed Interest Rate.** This offers a great measure of security to the home buyer. Your monthly mortgage payment will not change for the life of your loan. However, if the interest rates go below what you are paying, you may lose out unless you are able to re-negotiate or re-finance your mortgage. Be careful though and check before you re-negotiate. You may end up paying a lot of special charges such as "points." Your re-negotiation will depend on how long you've lived in your home, the amount of the rate, etc. Talk to your lender. Get a loan with no pre-payment penalties.

Fixed rate mortgages are typically set to have the amount of interest paid during the early years of your mortgage. You will then see a very slow decrease in the amount of principal you owe. After several years, this ratio will shift and you will be paying more of the principal.

Fixed rate loans are also available from non-conventional sources. You may be able to borrow from family, friends, the seller of the home you buy, or other parties willing to invest their money in a secure and solid investment. A friend of mine was able to find a fixed rate loan for part of his mortgage by finding a retired couple who wanted to invest the money they made from the sale of their home and have steady, secure monthly payments made directly to them. In this situation, you will still need to have proper paperwork and legal agreements drawn up. Your real estate agent, or escrow officer, will guide you through the process.

Another way to obtain a fixed rate loan is to assume an existing loan (if it is at a good rate for you) on the house of your dreams. The seller may be willing to get a cash down payment and carry the note himself or take a second mortgage on the home.

The second kind of conventional loan is the **Adjustable-rate Mortgage (ARM).** These were introduced in the home mortgage industry as a result of the inflation and instability of the interest rates in the late 1970's and early 1980's. The banks and other lending institutions were suffering financial losses as the interest rates of borrowing and lending moneys were rising and did not have a favorable spread for them.

The ARMs' interest rate varies according to government indexes.

Understand that the amount of total mortgage you can have depends on the interest rate. You cannot control the interest rates, but you can make wise decisions.

If the interest rates are high when you are buying a house, an adjustable rate is a good alternative. When the interest rate goes down, so does your monthly payments. The reverse is also true. Understand the caps, possible annual increase, and the total increase limits.

The higher the interest rate, the less house you can afford. If you are able to get a lower rate, you can afford a more expensive home. So, when you are looking at interest rates, a variable rate at 7.5% may be better than a fixed rate at 11.5%.

Lenders, however, need to insure themselves that when the rates on an ARM do go up, you will be able to pay the higher monthly payments. A lender may qualify you for an interest rate somewhere between the fixed and adjustable rates.

Look carefully at all the items and conditions of your adjustable rate loan. Note what national indicator you must consider on your loan, as well as the percentage your loan can go up at any given time.

You need to decide: Do you want the long-term stability of a fixed interest rate loan? Can you better deal with an initially lower rate that may go up later?

You can protect yourself against a large increase of interest rates. You can negotiate for a maximum amount that your payments can be increased. Such terms may be included in your agreement with the lender automatically. Understand them.

Keep in mind though that the lowest rate quoted to you may not be your best alternative. **APR's — annual percentage rates**, don't necessarily tell you the whole story.

Low rates sometimes come with higher "points." Each point is 1% of the total amount which is paid at the closing or before.

Let's look at some examples:

You want a loan for $150,000, at a 30 year fixed rate. One lender gives you a 9% loan with "no points." His APR is 9%. The other lender offers 8.5% with "three points," and his APR is 8.83%.

Which one is better?

Here is the calculation:

The payment on the first loan will be $1,206.93 a month — principal and interest. The payment on the second loan will be $1,153.37, which is $53.56 a month lower.

Now, figure in what it would take you to recoup the up-front 3% costs of the 8.5% loan: seven years for a total of $4,500. So, your 9% loan is cheaper on a no cash up front basis for the first seven years. If you would be selling or refinancing on the first seven years, the higher rate is better for you.

Even if you were able to deduct the $4,500 from your tax liability — you still will need about 4 1/2 years to recoup the up-front cost.(considering you are at the 36% bracket, deduct $1,620, leaving $2,880 of points to recoup.)

Also, in a few years, you may be able to find an 8% zero point loan, and you can refinance. It's tough if you already laid out $4,500 up front. However, at zero point 9%, to go down to 8% zero points is a lot of savings. Don't wait for interest rates to go down. Move forward. You can refinance if it pays to do so.

Now, while we are on mortgage rates, let's go a step further and discuss adjustable-rate deals. A friend of mine had always opted for a fixed rate. He found the fixed rate at 9.25%, and first year ARM at 6.375%. My friend chose the latter because he saved $3,000 over the first year and he can invest it. Or he can use it to pay down the mortgage with extra payments.

ARM's are advantageous for people who stay in their homes only for a few years. In Arizona for example, 60% of all new home loans are ARM's — as reported by three of the largest banks.

A year ago, they reported 25% ARM's and 75% fixed rates. In 1994, they reported the reverse was true.

The range in interest rates vary by lenders. Some adjust at six month or one-year intervals. Some adjust monthly. Some are tied to 3, 5, or 7 years — and annually thereafter. The higher rate increases may start with a low, "teaser" rate.

Some ARM's also have caps for a period of time — not to exceed a certain percentage over the lifetime of the loan, or several years.

If you are a good investor, or know of one, the money you save the first couple of years can be invested or re-invested by paying off the mortgage.

Some banks offer good rates, free incentives, but you are required to keep the loan for a minimum number of years — or may have to pay a penalty. Ask for no penalty policy. You should be able to negotiate this.

Some banks offer a 48 hour **Pre-Approval** on a completed loan application.

Ask you loan officer or agent for advice. Consider the following points before you decide on a fixed loan or an ARM:

— If you will be in your home more than 5 years, should you stay with fixed rates? ARM's may be higher after that point.

— Stay on fixed rate loans if you are on a fixed income, your income will not increase significantly, or you are not comfortable with risks of the ARM.

— Stay on fixed rate loans if you prefer security.

— If you can assume risks, expect to stay in your home for a few years only, you can be better off with an ARM.

— Avoid ARM's that guarantee you will never pay over a certain dollar amount. What happens when the rates go up is that the interest being charged gets tacked onto the back of the loan, and your payments will be mostly interest.

— When you convert an ARM to a fixed rate you may be charged extra for converting.

Here are some guidelines for ARM loans:

1. Make sure you can keep up with rate increase.

2. Understand how your mortgage payments fluctuate.

3. Get a cap on the interest rate.

4. Avoid caps on monthly mortgage payments.

5. Find out how long your original, low rate will last.

6. Find out what is involved in converting the ARM to a fixed rate.

Government Loans

This type of loan includes the FHA (Federal Housing Administration) loans and VA (Veterans' Administration, or GI) loans.

Usually, banks do not like to negotiate FHA or VA loans. However, a government guarantee, and your ability to qualify makes it a great loan on an almost non-risk basis for the lender.

A lender may charge a few extra percentages (points) on FHA or VA loans. It is a one-time only charge.

FHA insures the loan, so the lender will accept a smaller down payment, as little as 3%-5%. This is helpful for new home buyers with little cash for down payment.

FHA loans are assumable. This means that if there is an existing FHA loan on a home, you can take over payments. Or, if you get an FHA approved loan, when you sell your home, the buyer will be able to assume your loan. This is very attractive for buyers and sellers. You may still have to qualify to take over the existing loan.

On FHA loans, you can prepay without penalties.

The drawbacks for FHA loans are the following:

1. You are required to pay mortgage insurance premiums (MIP) up front. If you borrow this amount, your monthly payments are higher. However, if you can put 20% down payment or maybe put down the proceeds from the sale of your last home, the FHA waves the insurance premium. The seller can also pay these points by packing them into the purchase price. However, the property may not meet the appraisal when the purchase price is inflated to include the points.

2. An FHA appraiser must appraise your purchase. If repairs are needed, FHA may require the repairs before approval of the loan. The seller may not be willing to make repairs.

3. FHA approves loans only up to a certain figure; it depends on the area.

4. FHA loans must be paid to the end of the month, not to the date of pay-off when you sell your home.

As of this year, it has gotten easier to qualify for an FHA loan. The FHA officials have stated that "unnecessary barriers" have been removed for people whose debt ratios don't fit the standard ones but who are good credit risks. They have also eased property fixing requirements and put FHA loans into the computers of lending institutions — making loan approval time much less. The government can help you get a loan.

What does this mean to you?

1. Your local lender can look at your debt ratio, taking into consideration many items that show you are a good risk — such as never missed a rent payment, never late in payments, can handle a higher than typical debt ratio.

2. The income you are expected to earn in 3 years instead of the typical 5 years will be considered. Full time employment also no longer means a 40 hour week.

3. Child-care expenses are not included in recurring monthly debts, realizing that when child care is high, families find alternatives ways.

4. Cash accumulated from community-based or family-based "savings-club" will not be seen as a loan to be repaid.

5. Only property repair that is essential for safety and soundness will be considered enforceable.

VA loans are guaranteed by the Veteran's Administration. These are available to any veteran who served 190 active days since September 16, 1940; or any veteran who had at least 90 days of service during a war. If you enlisted after September 7, 1980, you must have at least 2 years' service.

You also need an honorable discharge if you are no longer with the military. ROTC members may qualify. You must live in your purchased home and have the home pass a VA appraisal.

VA loans are attractive for the following reasons:

1. You can get a home with little or no money down payment.

2. They provide competitive interest rates and lower closing costs.

3. You can get a VA loan up to $184,000. Check this amount, it can change.

4. You can prepay the loan without penalty.

5. The loan is assumable.

In a VA loan, you can expect to pay discount points, appraisal fees, VA funding fee. These expenses can be paid by the seller to help you get in for zero down. This usually results in a higher price and makes it more difficult for the property to meet the appraisal.

VA & FHA loan information resources are provided in the appendix. Write to them for more details.

SELLER FINANCING

Seller Financing is the next type of loan. The seller of your home may be able to finance your purchase at an attractive rate. Professional investors may also be available.

Sellers may be willing to finance your loan especially if they do not need to cash-out their home, or own it free and clear. Sellers who are retiring may want the tax benefits of small increments of monthly income extended over the period of the loan. They may (if they are older) want to negotiate a 15 year balloon payment. At that time, you may pay the total owed, or renegotiate. More on this in a later chapter.

If the seller finances your loan, you will need to provide the financial information required by him or her. Obviously, seller financed homes do not fall in the pre-approval category.

My suggestion is: get **pre-approved** from a lending institution and have your letter of commitment. If you find your dream home and the seller will carry your loan at favorable terms, then you can negotiate. You are approaching it from a strong standpoint.

Being **pre-approved** gives you emotional strength. It is money in the bank! It gives you power to negotiate for what you want with the lender, agents, sellers. **It gives you power to buy now and get a BETTER DEAL.**

OTHER FORMS OF FINANCING

There are other, "creative" ways of financing the purchase of your home. Your agent or lender can explain these in more detail if you are interested. Here are some examples:

1. Combine seller and conventional financing. Get the lender (bank, etc.) to give you, for example, 80% of the total purchase price and have the seller finance the balance, or whatever balance after the down payment. The first lender gives you the First Mortgage, and the seller carries the Second Mortgage. Second Mortgages are subordinate to First Mortgages.

Second mortgages may be at a higher interest rate than the bank's, and of shorter duration when borrowed from lending institutions. Negotiate the interest rate on your second mortgage and the terms such as length of loan, no payoff penalty, extension of loan if needed in an emergency, etc.

2. A second mortgage can also be obtained from a private lender.

3. You can assume an existing loan. Check the documents because some loans are due on sale.

4. You can borrow from a private lender: You may need to put a down payment and borrow the rest. A large down-payment makes this a good risk since the money invested and the value of the property provide ample security for the lender.

5. You can borrow a part of the selling price from the seller. Some lenders will not approve you for a loan if you are not putting some cash in the transaction. Others may increase the prime rate or points. Some lenders have mortgage loans specifically to allow you to borrow your down payment. There are two ways to assume a seller loan:

- Assume with qualifying. You must make application with the lender and qualify. The interest rate may be increased.

- Assume without qualifying — where the seller is responsible.

6. FMHA Mortgages are available for low or moderate income borrowers in rural areas. Check with the Farmer's Home Administration for qualifying information (see appendix for address and details). This usually offers very little or no money down and very low interest rates.

FMHA also guarantees loans like FHA & VA loans. Check for details.

7. Lease with Option to Buy is another way to finance your home. This is good especially if you have no cash for down payment.

8. Management Agreement with Option to Buy

9. Sale-Leaseback

10. Trade-in Property

11. Exchange Property

12. Wraparound Mortgage

13. Limited Partnership

14. Direct Personal or Commercial loan

15. Life Estate

16. Refinance on Purchase

17. Line of Credit from your own bank or Bank loan

Chapter 5

Find The Right Financing For You

"Money is like a sixth sense without which you cannot make a complete use of the other five."

— W. Somerset Maugham (1915)

In this chapter we will discuss some particulars of financing your Dream Home.

You may find an attractive home with financing available through the seller, or an assumable loan. You haven't wasted your time in going to a lender and getting pre-approved.

Pre-approval gives you choice, options, and a comfort zone. So, no matter what you are expecting, go to your lender first. Your **pre-approval** letter places you in control of the home buying process. **It gives you power to buy NOW!**

Getting financing you can live with is very important. If you have already figured out your income and expenses, you know what you can afford to pay every month. Getting the financing you want will help you enjoy your home even more by removing the stress and tension that many people feel when they are stretched to the limit.

THE KEY PLAYERS IN LENDING

1. The **Loan Officer** is your contact person at the lending institution that you select. The loan officer will take all your financial information and keep coming back for more as needed. Be sure that when you meet with this person you have as much information as you can. This will speed up the pre-approval process. See the list of items you will need at the end of this chapter.

If your lender requires any other information, the loan officer will let you know. Don't be discouraged or overwhelmed. Sometimes you may feel like you are running around like crazy getting papers! It will be worth it. Although there are non-qualifying loans that require less paperwork, these are at a higher rate of interest and require larger down payments.

Organize yourself early. Remember that lending institutions have strict rules and regulations. They need official written documentation to all your financial information.

2. The **Loan Processor** — will process your loan. The loan processor will make sure all the legal and financial requirements are met and will get the credit report, and later the appraisal on your home.

3. The **Underwriter** decides whether or not you get the loan.

CRITERIA FOR GETTING PRE-APPROVED

When your application is completed, all the information must be verified: employment, credit history, income, etc.

The lender will also look for your payment history, such as are you prompt? Late in payment? If you have a lot of credit cards and have lots of credit available on them, it could be a tempting sign for your lender.

As I recommended earlier, get a credit report, clean out any problem areas, pay off as much as possible, and don't run new debts during the loan process. A second credit report is typically ordered prior to closing and your new debts will show up. Also, make sure you have on record any letters of explanation if you had previously run into credit problems.

A friend of mine was going to medical school on student loans. When he was in his residency, he and his wife ran into financial difficulties and overlooked prompt payments on the student loans. Before applying for a home loan, they made sure they had letters of explanation on record as to why their difficulties. It took over three months to have all the paperwork in place. So, start now if you need to clean up your credit report.

To approve your loan, lenders look for the following:

1. Can you repay? They will look at your entire financial record to determine this.

2. Do you have a good credit history? This means are you the kind of person who honors your debts?

3. Do you have assets that will help collect the moneys owed? Can you afford a down payment? If you have to borrow the down payment, this counts as a loan as well. If your down payment is your saved earnings or a gift from someone, it is better.

4. What do you have for collateral? Typically, your house is your collateral. The lender will make sure that your house is worth what you are paying.

LETTER OF COMMITMENT

When your loan is approved, you will get a letter of commitment from the lender that includes:

1. the total loan amount

2. the length of the loan (15 years, 30 years typically)

3. points charged

4. interest rate and how calculated

5. monthly payment

Now you have a set amount of time to sign and close the agreement. When you sign, you have agreed to the terms.

INTEREST RATES

Interest rates change daily. You will have to decide if you want to lock in today's rate, or let it float.

If you lock into a rate, you are guaranteed that rate even if it goes up. The time is limited for locking in rates, so check with your lender.

UP FRONT FEES

A lender can charge fees to process your loan and give you a loan.

The first is "points" which is a single percentage of the total loan amount. These are in addition to your loan and must be paid in cash. Or there may be no "points" charged.

The second is the "loan fee" which is charged to process the paperwork. The amount varies, so ask.

If you know your credit problems, tell your loan officer up front. It will help you clean up these problems. However, if you are denied a loan, the lender must tell you why in writing. You could be re-considered if you repair the problem. A good loan officer will work with you and let you know what you need to do.

You have to be before you can do.

Consider discussing with the lender what you need to do to repair your situations and do it. You can also consider applying through a mortgage company that deals with hard-to-place loans. They take bigger risks, charge higher interest rates. But, they are under the criteria set by large lending institutions that include the government. Sometimes, getting your Dream Home may mean higher payments to get you started.

Pre-approval has a charm here because you will know just what you can spend for a house. You don't have to go out and find a home, fall in love, **then** get a loan. That's too frustrating. Instead, a **pre-approved** loan will tell you just what you can afford. If you have made your dream list and know what you **want**, you can match your Dream & your loan!

My friend's daughter bought a $30,000 car in 30 minutes. The auto industry — Detroit — makes it easy for a buyer to buy: easy, simple, fast financing.

Yet the same woman does not know how to buy a home and get easy, simple financing, because of the mystique of the complex mortgage loan process.

My friend's niece called him the other day needing some mortgage advice. She and her husband bought a $24,000 home three years ago, fixed it up, made other improvements and just sold it for $67,000. They found their Dream Home. The asking price was $143,000. They got pre-approved, had their pre-approval letter, offered $128,000. The offer was accepted. Now they had to decide on a 30 year fixed mortgage at 8 3/4% or a 6% ARM with one point annual increase cap with a cap of 6% maximum. That is in her market. The rate varies from market to market. What do you think my friend advised her to do? You can figure it out. Your mortgage banker and real estate agent can help you with these decisions. Take a careful look at what you will be saving and what you will be paying over several years.

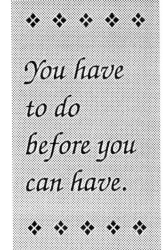

You have to do before you can have.

Also consider taking a few months and clearing out your credit, paying off outstanding debts, working hard, and don't forget: visualizing your Dream Home. Then, go back again. Don't give up! A Winning Formula — Ability and Effort = Results

My motto is, do whatever it takes, that is moral and legal, to get your Dream Home.

Take with you to the lender as much of following that you have:

1. Two years' tax documents

2. Check stubs for this year and W-2's for last two years

3. List of all income (use worksheet in appendix and take with you)

4. List of all expenses (using worksheet)

5. Letters from your employer regarding any regular payments you receive in addition to your salary (regular bonuses, commission, etc.)

6. Documents indicating judgments entitling you to receive alimony, child support, settlements, etc.

7. Your credit report that you ordered earlier and put in good condition

8. Copies of all bank statements for your savings and checking accounts for the past three months. If you have a large deposit during the past few months, you will need to explain the sources.

9. Copies of all assets in stocks, life insurance, etc.

10. Names and addresses of past employers, landlords, and lending institutions if you have outstanding loans (home, business, etc.)

11. If self-employed, include profit and loss statements for past two years and year-to-date

12. Application fee, and other fees the lender will need up front.

13. Addresses for past five to ten years of residences

14. Copies of your rent checks for past one year

15. Copy of your listing agreement if you are selling your present home or, if sold, copy of purchase agreement

There are loans available that a home buyer can get with zero percent down. 90% of the loan is given by the lender and 10% plus closing costs loaned by another lender or seller or anyone else who takes a second position. Such loans can be at a higher interest rate.

There are also "non-conforming" loans for people who have a bad credit or bad past credit. Check all types of available loans and find one that fits your situation.

Chapter 6

Do I Need A Real Estate Agent?

"The reward of a thing well done is to have done it."

— Emerson (1844)

Finding a Real Estate agent should not be a problem. Finding the right one who will work with you and support you in your home needs is a **bit more work.**

If, for any reason, you do not like your agent, LEAVE. Find another one. Don't waste your time. This is important.

Let's first look at real estate terms when it comes to agents:

1. BROKER

A broker has been licensed by the State to conduct a real estate business. He is the boss, around which often agents work. A broker can be part of a franchise (Coldwell Banker for example) or he can have an independent office. A broker can work with you, or have his agents work with you.

A well known real estate name does not guarantee sources of a great agent. Each office is independently operated, and its quality depends on the work done by the agents.

Select a firm, or agent based on reputation, word of mouth, and your gut feeling after interviewing an agent.

2. AGENTS

An agent can be an independent contractor or an employee. He works for a **broker.** He is the most likely to deal with your, show you homes. He is your salesman.

When an agent puts a house on the market, he is getting the listing and is called a *listing agent.* An agent is called a sub agent when he is the one showing you a house and handling you, the buyer.

3. REALTOR®

A Realtor® with the trademark is an agent or broker who is affiliated with the NAR — National Association of Realtors. The NAR has a code of ethics that is beyond the specific state's laws. The MLS — Multiple Listings System, which lists all houses for sale is sponsored by Realtors.

Let me give you a brief description of an MLS listing.

Most homes listed on the market are listed in the computer system known as MLS. MLS listings have specific formats that give you simple data about the house, such as:

— Address

— Listing price

— Locations of property — town, area, township, lot number, map coordinates

— type and size of rooms:

— LR — living room

— GR — great room

— DR — dining room

— KT — kitchen

— FR — family room

— MB — master bedroom

— #B — # of bedrooms total

— The mortgage:

— 1M — 1st mortgage

— 1P — 1st mortgage payment

— taxes, tax year, school district, and assumption information

— Directions to home, other property information

— Description of property

— style of house

— total number of rooms

— exterior and interior styling

— The listing agent information

Your agent will pull this information from what you tell him. This is why I had you do your dream list, your priorities, your wish list. The more specific you can be with your agent, the better able she or he will be in the search. You will get a printout of each listing.

4. BUYER'S AGENT

An agent who represents you, or a **Buyer's Agent** assures you that you have good representation on your side. This person will conduct all negotiations with your interest in mind. He will keep your confidential information and will negotiate on your behalf. He can also give you tips and recommendations on price, down payment, terms, etc.

Your agent is paid in a number of ways. It all depends on the agreement you have with him. Here are some ways your agent gets paid:

1) He makes one-half of the commission on the purchase price of the house and subsequently splits it (or keeps a certain percentage) with his broker.

2) A flat fee based on the purchase price.

3) A retainer fee that may be applied to the total fee.

4) You or the seller may pay a fee.

Use the charts and questionnaires in this chapter to evaluate the agent with whom you want to work.

Dream List

QUESTIONS TO ASK YOUR AGENT

1. How much will I pay you for your services?

2. What services do I pay for?

3. Do you require a retainer?

4. Who pays the commission? Seller? Buyer?

5. What are the terms of the exclusivity agreement?

6. What kinds of services can I expect from you?

There are many things you need to know from your agent. Sometimes, the seller may reduce the price of the house to cover his commission. Or, the seller may pay the commission. What we want here is to help you buy your Dream House spending as little of your money as possible.

Chart 6-1 Agent Questions

5. DUAL AGENCY

You may also have a **Dual Agency** when the listing agent and buyers agent work for the same company. You should be made aware of this.

You will probably be asked to sign **one of two** agreements once you decide to work with an agent:

1) Buyer's Agency Selection Form — when you select a buyer's agent.

2) Dual Agency Disclosure Agreement — when you and the seller grant the agent to represent both of you.

6. DISCOUNT BROKER

A **Discount Broker** gives you access to the MLS listings. You do the work yourself, such as

— get the listings

— see the homes

— draw up contracts

— arrange financing

❖ ❖ ❖ ❖ ❖

Horse sense is having good, stable knowledge.

You pay part of the commission. So, be sure that you know clearly what the broker will do and for what you are responsible, including any changes.

These are the six typical kinds of agents. Even seasoned buyers use agents. It is worth the effort, in my opinion. Home markets change year-to-year and you may not be aware of these changes.

Some agents are very experienced and really know the ins and outs. Some are new and less experienced, but have a good feel for the home market.

A friend of mine bought a home from an agent who was only in the business for one year. The agent had a good feel for the home market, and had good people sense. The agent was able to match the buyer and a home in a very short time. Her intuitive keenness gives her an edge over other, more experienced agents.

Another agent was so negative and difficult that she immediately told the buyers that they would probably not qualify and just go and buy a condo, or rent for a while. She did not know that my friends had cash in their pocket and were ready to buy! She lost out on a good deal!

When you first meet with an agent, use your agent questionnaire and also use your intuition. Your gut feeling should tell you if you like this person. You will be spending a lot of hours being driven from one house to another. The agent will become your friend and know more about you than most of your friends! So trust your instincts. If you don't like the person, go elsewhere. They all have access to the same multiple listing service.

Here are things you can expect from your agent:

- Your agent can help you match your financial capabilities with the house you want. Tell the agent frankly what you want to spend. You should know exactly what your pre-approved credit is by now. You have your pre-approval letter. Also, you know how much money you have for down payment.

- Your agent will tell you what is the estimated additional costs you will incur, such as closing costs, inspection, etc.

- Your agent will be able to estimate for you what your likely monthly payments be on your home. When agents are well versed in your area, they will know the approximate amount for utilities, taxes, and other expenses you will incur. In addition, your agent will be able to estimate your monthly mortgage payments.

- Your agent will help you find the best way to finance your home should you still not be pre-approved. Your agent can also help you find a lender if you have not been pre-approved.

    As I suggested at the beginning of this book, get **pre-approved**. I can't recommend this strongly enough. You should get your **pre-approval letter** before looking. Become a cash buyer now. A couple I know were pre-approved for $300,000. Even though they will not be buying a house for $300,000, they have the money; they are much more confident and able to negotiate anything they want.

• Your agent will help you find the right home. Here, your pre-planning of your dream home will make this process a pleasant one. Go to your agent with your lists, priorities, and have a frank discussion. Tell her or him what your needs are, desires, particular talents to fix a house, re-decorate, etc.

I know a single woman who was looking for a home. She wanted to spend about $110,000 and knew exactly what she wanted, but failed to tell her agent that she is not the kind to get a "fixer upper." After months of searching in the below $110,000 range, looking at all sorts of homes that could have used a bit of work, the agent suggested they look at a bit more expensive home, older, but completely remodeled. The friend said fine, and pulled out all her assets. She was able to find a $130,000 home, fully clean, painted, carpeted, ready to move in. The extra cost was well worth the peace of mind and fitted her needs perfectly. Her agent knew my friend's tastes and capabilities, and was able to match a home and a buyer. She had a pre-approval letter for a $125,000 mortgage and only had to come up with a $5000 down payment and closing costs.

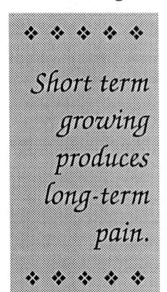

Short term growing produces long-term pain.

Another friend bought a home that was in a special category of "fixer-upper." She also is a single woman, who has an exceptional ability to take a "piece of junk" and turn it into a most charming home. Her house looked like a chicken coop — on a beautiful piece of property. This little "fixer" turned into a charming, cottage-like home. It took effort, imagination, talent, lots of guts, and stamina. If you have these abilities, then go for it. Be careful though and be very clear about what you can and cannot do!

• An agent will also give you information about your prospective community. Some agents have a packet of information listing schools, statistics, colleges, libraries, activities, temperatures, medical help, police, etc. These are really helpful. I sent a packet to a friend who was moving to the United States from South Africa and it proved to be useful information.

- An agent will present your offer to the seller. He will draw-up the agreement, list all the terms, and represent you. He will be able to tell you what the sale price was for comparable homes in the area.

- An agent will help you through the "paper-pushing" process and help you close the deal.

THE BEST AGENT

A word of advise: Don't immediately sign up with an agent; wait until you are sure.

Find an agent who is really active in, and knows, the neighborhood you want. In view of the experts in real estate, an active agent should be carrying a minimum of six listings in any period.

Notice if the agent has good people skills and can present you well. Beware of agents who make all kinds of claims and talk like they know everything. You will be dealing with a big ego and that always gets in the way.

Ask your friends. Check the agent's background. Get a feel for the firm and the agents who work there. Ask the local real estate board for any problems or complaints.

HOW MOST BUYERS CHOOSE AN AGENT

Most buyers choose an agent in one of three ways:

1. The agent answered the telephone when the buyer called about an ad. Some of the best agents are too busy to sit in an office to answer telephones.

2. The agent's name was on the sign. Just because an agent has a listing, it doesn't mean he is competent. Typically the agent who has a property listed cannot negotiate a better purchase for you than someone from another company.

3. The agent was met at an open house. Many top agents don't do open houses.

RULES OF THUMB IN PICKING THE RIGHT AGENT

1. All real estate agents are not alike. Like most sales industries, 20% of the people make 80% of the sales. You want to work with one of the 20% who make things happen.

2. It is better to work with a great salesperson from an average company than an average salesperson from a great company. It's the salesperson who helps you, not the company.

3. An agent who belongs to the "million dollar" club is not necessarily a top agent. In most marketplaces today, it takes less than 10 transactions within a year to qualify for the "million dollar club." Top agents typically close 25-100 transactions a year!

4. An agent who looks broke, probably is broke. The agent obviously has not helped many people to buy or sell homes. He can't help you either. You can tell a lot by the person's dress, auto, brochures, computerization, etc.

5. If the agent doesn't have a cellular phone, forget it. Every pro does.

6. If an agent is reluctant to tell you how many transactions he did last year, chances are it wasn't many. An agent who hasn't helped many others won't help you either.

7. Typically, you will seldom find top agents sitting in the office answering telephones or sitting at open houses. They are too busy working with buyers.

8. Typically, an agent who is not working with anyone, helps no one. A busy agent always finds time to help a serious buyer.

9. An agent who is new but aggressive, knowledgeable, well dressed, communicates well, shows a desire to work extra hard and weekends can be a better choice than most veterans.

WHAT YOU WANT THE AGENT TO DO FOR YOU

You want to have the following points of understanding with your agent:

1. You do not want to miss anything. Therefore, the agent must agree to inform you of any new properties in the neighborhoods you've selected within 24 hours of submission to the MLS.

2. Agrees to provide the sales records of all properties sold within the selected neighborhoods in the last year.

3. Provide you with a number of properties on the market (within the MLS) for a year ago, 6 months ago, 3 months ago, today. This gives you the market trend.

4. Will represent you, not the seller.

5. Will present your purchase agreement personally to the seller and state your position (whenever possible).

6. Agrees to show you FSBO's (For Sale By Owner Properties).

7. Direct you to a lender who will **Pre-Approve** your loan (not pre-qualify) before you buy.

8. Will provide you information on the selected neighborhood, such as schools, Home Owner Association terms, Public Transportation, etc.

9. Be willing to search for homes in your price range in neighborhoods above your price range.

Dream List

AGENT QUESTIONS

1. What is the firm's reputation?

2. What is the agent's specialty?

3. How long has the agent lived and worked in the area?

4. Is the support staff friendly?

5. Does the agent return your calls promptly?

6. Does the agent have a calm and friendly personality?

7. Does the agent seem like he knows his business?

8. Can you see the agent's resume?

9. How many properties has he listed this past year?

10. How many sold?

11. Does your agent take time with you or is he in a hurry?

12. Is your agent organized?

13. Does your agent listen to you?

14. Do the houses you look at match what you told the agent?

15. Does your agent show you houses listed mostly with his firm?

16. What real estate courses has the agent taken lately?

Chart 6-2 Agent Questions

Dream List

AGENT CHECKLIST

Here is a checklist for choosing the right agent. The agent you select should score the highest. But if the agent does not score at least 10 points, keep looking.

1. Good experience with agent in past sale or purchase. (5 points)_____

2. Agent is highly recommended by someone I trust.   (5 points)_____

3. The company which the agent works for is highly recommended by someone I trust.   (2 points)_____

4. Agrees to work as the Buyer's Agent.   (5 points)_____

5. Got recommendation from lender or title company. (2 points)_____

6. Agent has closed 25 transactions within the last year.
                                                       (5 points)_____

7. The agent is new but is aggressive, knowledgeable, well dressed, communicates well, shows desire to work extra hard and on weekends.
                                                       (5 points)_____

8. Says to you "Let me know if you see something you like and I'll help you."   (–5 points)_____

9. Willing to show you FISBO's.   (3 points)_____

10. After interviewing three, your "gut" tells you this agent is the right one.   (3 points)_____

11. Agrees to fulfill all your reasonable requirements. (3 points)_____

Total_____

Chart 6-3 Agent Checklist

If you don't like an agent, you can let him go as soon as your 30-60 day exclusivity contract is up. Or, tell the agent it is really not a good working situation for you and you need to stop wasting his time. If an agent showed you a particular listing, you need to know you cannot buy the same home from another agent.

SALE-BY-OWNER

If a house is listed FSBO (For Sale By Owner), you can still have an agent represent you.

If you decide to buy directly without using an agent, be careful and get professional help, especially on these deals. Even if you know what you're doing, still have an attorney check your contracts before you sign them.

Especially, make sure your home is completely inspected and all documents are thoroughly verified.

Chapter 7

Why You Need A Real Estate Agent

"The ornament of a house is the friends who frequent it."

— Emerson (1870)

Of all the properties listed for sale, 90% are handled by real estate agents. Without using an agent, it is impossible to view these properties.

Not all properties sold through Realtors® are good values, nor are all properties sold through sellers good values. If you look at the ratio, of the 90% sold through Realtors®, as opposed to the 10% sold by sellers direct we find that 90% of the good values will be handled by Realtors®, as opposed to 10% of the good values sold through sellers.

By limiting yourself only to properties sold by sellers direct, you could be limiting yourself to only 10% of the good values. It is not your goal to eliminate the real estate agent or necessarily to eliminate a commission, but it is your goal to get a good value.

A good value is a good value whether a real estate agent or a commission is involved. Without the use of a real estate agent, you miss out on 90% of the properties on the market. Your primary reason for wanting to use a real estate agent therefore is to get exposure to these properties. The real estate agent will be your ally in helping to secure your American Dream.

HOW MANY AGENTS DO I NEED?

Some people believe if one agent can help, several might be better.

It has been my experience, in years of working with buyers, that through the process of looking for a property, most buyers are operating under fear. A buyer's greatest fear is the fear of loss. Buyers are afraid of missing out on something — missing out on their Dream Home; missing out on a good value; missing out on the right property for their family. As a result, most buyers believe that the more agents they work with, the greater chance of not missing something.

Buyers feel they'll get better exposure by looking in a newspaper, driving the streets, looking for signs, and working with several agents. However, this type of thinking is wrong. Thinking like this will actually cause you to miss out on properties.

The best way to get exposed to the properties in the marketplace is to create a working relationship with **one good agent**.

WHERE ARE THE GOOD VALUES?

Buyers work hard looking in the newspaper and home magazines for properties for sale. But in a city with 2000 properties for sale, there might only be 200-300 properties advertised in the newspaper in a particular week. Many of the properties are advertised two or three different times within the week so, in reality, there are even fewer properties advertised than the number of ads.

The same applies to homes magazines. If 2000 properties are for sale, home magazines may list only 200-300 properties.

What about the rest of the properties? What about the ones that never get advertised? Many of these are good values.

You may think that the good values are either or will be found in the home magazines. Keep in mind that a real good value doesn't need to be advertised. Every good agent is working with perhaps five to ten buyers on a monthly basis at any one given time. Their advertising efforts are directed to attract buyers, not necessarily to sell homes because you can't sell homes without buyers.

Ads are written to attract as many buyers as possible. Once the agents get the buyers, they direct them to the right properties. Therefore, certain ads are written over and over again to attract calls, rather than to sell the properties.

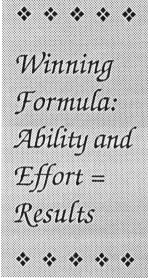

Winning Formula: Ability and Effort = Results

In a marketplace where there are approximately 2000 homes for sale, as many as 200 new properties can go on the market in any given week. It would be a nightmare for real estate agents continually to write new ads day after day after day just to advertise these properties for sale. Again, what they do is to run ads that consistently attract buyer calls and then they direct those buyers to properties. Ads can also be written on properties to appease sellers who feel that if their property is advertised, it will help sell it.

If a property is a good value an ad is not needed for it. You don't have to write an ad to attract a buyer for a good value. They merely take those buyers to the properties the instant they are listed and those properties are sold before they are ever advertised.

Even if a company planned to place an ad on a property, by the time that ad is written or placed, the good values are already gone.

Many buyers will drive streets with "For Sale" signs on them or go into Open Houses. Keep in mind that there are many sellers who don't wish to have a sign on their property. Some neighborhoods don't even allow signs on properties. As competitive as the real estate industry is for a real estate agent, when an agent gets a real good value on the market, many times he will purposely withhold placing a sign on that property for several days, even weeks, hoping to keep the activity level down for a while so he has a chance to sell it himself and double his commission. By the time a sign is eventually placed, or an ad is eventually written and placed on those properties, they are already sold.

I took a call one day at my office on a property that I had listed. The buyer said to me on the phone, "We have been driving this street every day looking for homes for sale, we just saw this sign go on this property today. There must be some mistake, the sign already says SOLD." I had to inform these buyers that this property had been on the market for several weeks and the seller requested that no sign be placed on their property. However, after the property had already been sold, we placed our sign with a SOLD sign on it to help with the listing of other properties in that neighborhood.

Again, It doesn't take a sign or an ad to sell a property, it takes a buyer. When companies advertise, they are advertising results — not advertising properties.

Remember, it is your goal to find a good value. A good value doesn't have to be advertised to be sold. A good value doesn't have to have a sign on it to be sold. A good value can be sold without a sign and without an ad. To stay on top of the good values, and find yourself a good home, you must be in contact with a good real estate agent.

HOW MANY AGENTS DO I NEED?

Buyers also make the mistake of thinking that the more agents they stay in contact with, the better chance of finding the right values. One might logically think that since good values don't have to be advertised to be sold; a sign doesn't have to placed on them to be sold; all that is needed is an agent who knows about them; then therefore, it is.

This is one of the biggest mistakes that you can make. The more agents you talk to, the greater chance of missing something. Real estate agents work with many buyers at once. Many of these buyers are looking for the same type of property. When a good value comes on the market, which buyer do you think the agent contacts first about a particular property? The buyer working with several agents or the buyer who is working closely with him?

It is in your best interest to have a close, working relationship with an agent who can help you find a property. The more committed you are to working with a particular agent, the more committed the agent will be to help you locate the right home and let you know about a good value immediately. One agent committed to helping you locate the right property is better than a bunch of agents who aren't committed. It is in your best interest to have a close, working relationship with the agent showing you properties. Let that agent know that you will work only with him. Because of this, the agent will be motivated to keep you informed before other buyers.

The agent makes just as much money selling you another company's property as he will selling his own company's property. So you do not have to call the company that has the sign or an ad on the property. The agent you are working with will be able to show you any property. As a matter of fact, there is actually a disadvantage in buying a property from an agent who has the property listed for sale. If an agent is working as a buyers' agent, in many instances when he shows his own company's listings, he must work with you as a disclosed, dual agent. However, an agent working with you as a buyers' agent, when showing another company's listing will still be working as only your agent in that particular transaction.

Real estate agents are paid on a commission basis. They are given no draws, no salaries. Their time is the only stock they have in their trade. Most real estate agents fear spending weeks or months helping a couple in finding the right property only to have them buy it through another agent. It is like working a job for a couple of months and not getting paid. Unless a buyer is willing to commit to an agent, few agents are willing to provide the dedicated service necessary to help that buyer locate the right property.

There is no need for you to duplicate your efforts with so many real estate agents. You don't have to call the company with the sign; you don't have to call the company with the ad in the paper. Every broker has the same information on every property for sale. That information can be given readily to you by one agent. That same agent can show you any property. Should you decide on a property, the same price and terms can be negotiated through an agent who does not have the listing as with one who does have the listing. In addition, if an agent knows that you are going to work with him he would have a motivation even to do cold calling in the neighborhoods you want to try to dig up properties for sale that could be right for you.

CAN I BUY DIRECT FROM THE SELLER?

Many buyers think that avoiding the real estate agent and trying to buy a home directly through the seller is to their advantage. They believe that they are saving a commission. In my 20 some years of being in the real estate business, I found that most For Sale By Owners are typically overpriced. This is not to say that such homes could not be a good buy. However, the majority of good buys are offered by Realtors®. Therefore, in order to insure that you get the best value you can, you need to work with a licensed real estate agent to get the exposure to all the good values in the market place.

Here is how the real estate industry works. The lifeblood of the real estate industry is listings. When a seller agrees to sell his home with the real estate company, he has given that company a listing of his property. Within the listing, the sellers have agreed to pay the real estate company a commission for the marketing and selling of his property. The commission is not paid until the property is sold. 95% of all listings taken today in the real estate industry are taken on an exclusive basis. This means that the listing company is entitled to the commission when the property sells regardless of who sells it. Companies take properties on an exclusive basis in order to insure the return on investment in advertising and marketing for the sale of the property.

To get a property sold, brokers will enlist the help of other brokers in the community to sell the property. This is done through a cooperation agreement or through Multiple Listing Service. Real estate brokers will typically split the commission that they will receive 50/50 with the broker who sells the property. In essence, you have a selling broker and a listing broker. This creates two sides of a transaction, a selling side and a listing side. The commission is split between selling side and the listing side.

Real estate companies and brokers hire **real estate agents** on an independent contractor basis to take listings and sell properties. They split their commissions with their agents on a 50/50 or greater basis.

When an agent lists the property, he receives 50% or more of the **listing** side of the commission when the property sells. If that agent were to sell the property he lists, he or she will also receive a percentage of the selling side of the commission which is typically 50% or greater. The amount that an agent is paid by his or her broker is dependent on the agreement made by that broker and the agent. Typically that commission can be 50% all the way up to 100% of that commission depending on the arrangement and bonus plans of the broker involved.

Therefore, if an agent listed and sold the same property, he'll receive 50% or more of the selling side of the commission and 50% or more of the listing side of the commission. If another agent within the same company sells the particular listing, he will receive a percentage of the selling side of the commission. The percentage that the agent would receive for selling his own company's listings is typically no different than the percentage that he'd receive for selling another company's listing.

The important point here is that since an agent receives approximately the same money or commission for selling his company's listing or another company's listing, there is no disadvantage in using that particular agent in showing all properties. The agent's real motivation is to find the buyer a home. An agent is motivated by earning his fees or commissions, earning his living. So you are going to use the agent to find your American Dream Home. All other purposes for using the real estate agent are secondary to this point.

DOES THE AGENT REPRESENT ME?

You might be asking yourself, when I look for a home, who does the agent represent, me or the seller? Regardless of what a real estate agent may tell you, regardless of what disclosure document you may sign as to the representation, it is my recommendation that you pay homage to an old real estate term called "let the buyer beware." You should go into every real estate transaction looking out for your own best interest by assuming that all others, excluding your attorney, are representing their own best interest. If you go into each transaction with this in mind, you will limit your risks and problems.

Traditionally, when a real estate company took a listing, that company and every agent working with that company became the agent of the seller. Through the MLS, every cooperating broker signed an agreement that they were a sub-agent of the seller. A sub-agent has the same responsibilities that an agent has. Basically under agency law, an agent has a fiduciary responsibility to that party. He becomes their eyes, their nose, their ears, and their mouth. The agent works for the principal, which in this case would be the seller.

As an example, if you were to mention something that would increase the bargaining position of the seller, the agent would be obligated to relate this information to the seller, thus giving the seller bargaining position over you. In recent years, most states have created laws that obligate the real estate agent, prior to showing a buyer properties, to disclose to the buyer whom they represent in a transaction. This serves the buyer notice so a buyer will not disclose information he may not want the seller to find out.

Prior to these disclosure laws, it would seem that a buyer was at a tremendous disadvantage. However, practically speaking, it was actually the seller who was at the disadvantage. This is due to the fact that most agents had a tendency to work in the best interest of the party, whether it be a buyer or a seller, with whom they were working. If an agent was showing properties to a buyer and spending time with that buyer, the agent would have a tendency to work in the best interest of the buyer. In many cases, the agent would disclose confidential information about the seller to the buyer. As an example, it was quite common for an agent to say, "I think you can get a good buy on this property. These people have to sell; they are in financial trouble." Or, "These people are going to get divorced, you can get a good buy."

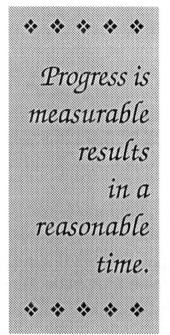

Progress is measurable results in a reasonable time.

In my opinion, prior to disclosure, it was actually the sellers who were at a disadvantage. Disclosure laws more than anything else taught the real estate agent the proper way to do business and put him on notice that his interaction with buyers and sellers may not be correct. This is not to say that the real estate agent would intentionally do something wrong, but due to a lack of knowledge of agency law, most real estate agents didn't really realize whom actually it was they represented, and what representing someone as an agent really meant.

Today more and more agents are representing buyers than ever before. Once an agent represents a buyer, he becomes the buyer's eyes, ears, nose and mouth and must work in the best interest of the buyer. That agent must do everything in his power to enhance your bargaining position.

So the question is, "Should I work with a buyer's agent?" The answer is not a simple one. In states where buyer representation is not common, you may have difficulty finding such an agent. Some of the best agents in town may be working with the company that does not permit its agents to work as a buyer's representative. Therefore, since our primary purpose in using a real estate agent is to locate a property, it may not be in your best interest to work with a buyer's representative in that particular town knowing that you may not have the best agent.

In other places, throughout America, buyer representation is extremely common and sometimes, as high as 100% of the agents showing properties work as the buyer's agents. The problem in these cases is finding the agent who understands what representing you really means.

We can solve both of these problems by realizing that our primary goal in working with an agent is to locate the right property and not to look at real estate agents primarily as your representative. Since a real estate agent's underlying goal is to earn a commission, sometimes things can be said to encourage a sale that may not totally represent your best interest. With this in mind, although it is my recommendation that you seek out an agent who will represent you in a transaction, it is also my recommendation that you, the buyer, beware and understand that even though the agent is saying that he is representing you, he may still not have a clear understanding as to what representing someone as an agent really means.

Always watch out for your best interest regardless of what disclosure documents have stated.

Keep in mind that a real estate company typically shows their own listings. In most instances, when an agent representing you shows you one of his or her own company's listings, in that transaction, the agent will be representing both you and the seller. Because of this, the fiduciary responsibility to both is limited. The agent cannot disclose to the seller what you might be willing to pay for the property or disclose anything that may enhance the seller's bargaining position. And likewise, the agent is not permitted to disclose anything to you that may enhance your bargaining position as to what a seller may take for a particular property. In those transaction, the agent is basically acting as a mediator in a transaction or as a facilitator in a transaction.

There are some companies who promote single agency representation wherein they will not represent both parties in a transaction. If their company has a listing, they will not show you their listings; they will recommend that you use another agency in looking at their company's listings and writing a transaction.

It is really in your best interest to find the right agent and work with that agent until you find the property. So working under the single agency situation is not practical because that agent who finds you a home may not end up selling you that property. That could complicate the issue.

So, even though representation is preferred, it is not the primary motivation. Be assured, that most agents are working in their best interest to earn a commission. In order to earn that commission, they must find you a home and that is the primary reason we want to use them to begin with. So looking at using a real estate agent with this perspective will benefit you the most and keep you out of trouble.

ADVANTAGES OF USING A BUYER'S AGENT

Here are the advantages of having an agent represent you, the buyer:

1. An agent or sub-agent of the seller is legally bound to represent the seller's best interest. As your agent, the agent will be legally bound to represent your best interest. The seller's agent must work to get the highest possible price and the best possible terms for the seller. As your agent, he must work to obtain the lowest possible price and the lowest possible terms.

2. The seller's agent is obligated to disclose any information that may enhance the seller's bargaining position, such as your financial position. However, if the agent is representing you, that agent must keep such information confidential. The seller's agent is also obligated to tell the seller about your urgency to buy or your willingness to improve your offer, or tell the seller about your financial position, or your plans to resell at a profit. However, if that agent is your agent, again such information must be kept in confidence.

3. If you are working with an agent who represents you, as a buyer, that agent can discuss information that may enhance your bargaining position, such as a seller's urgency to sell, their willingness to take less, whether the property is worth the asking price, or availability of like properties at a better price. He can discuss with you certain property features that may affect future marketability, and how other outside facts may lower property values. If you are working with an agent who represents the sellers, some of these discussions will never come up.

4. When it comes time to make your offer for purchase, although most real estate agents try to put together a purchase agreement to which all parties can agree, the agents who represent the seller will have a tendency to slant the agreement more to the seller's favor than to yours. If the agent is representing you, then the agreement will be slanted a little more in your favor.

5. Any agent, whether he represents you or the seller, can arrange property showings. Either can assist you in locating financing. Either agent can explain forms and agreements. However, a seller's agent may not readily point out disadvantages to you in an agreement. Both agents

can monitor escrows and counsel. Only the agent who represents you can keep your bargaining and financial position confidential. Only the agent who represents you can promote and protect your best interest. If you want an agent to negotiate the best terms for you, it must be one who represent you and not the seller.

6. Why should you have an agent represent you? It doesn't cost you any more. Some believe in order for an agent to represent you, the buyer must give the agent a commission. This is not true. Commission has nothing to do with agency relationships. How the commission is paid, whether the agent represents you or the seller, is going to be handled by the agent in what is typically common in the marketplace. In most areas, the seller pays the fee regardless of who the selling agent represents. In other areas, the buyer will pay his agent the fee and the seller will pay his agent the fee. The net result is the same. Here is an example:

When a seller lists his property, he agrees to pay a fee to the real estate company to sell his property, say 7% of the sale price of that property. When the property sells, the listing company is entitled to 7% of the sale price of that property. If another company sells that property, then that company agrees to split that 7% fee with the selling company: 3 1/2% retained by the listing company, and 3 1/2% goes to the selling company.

In some marketplaces, where buyer brokerage is not as common, when the sale is made, the listing company may elect to have the seller pay 3 1/2% of the sale price of the property and the buyer pay 3 1/2% directly to his agents. The total commission was 7% of the sale price. The money that the seller receives for the sale of his property is what he is going to use to pay the agent's fee. It is your money, regardless of how it is handled. If you give the buyer's agent 3 1/2% of the sale price, and the other 96 1/2% of the sale price is given to the seller, who in turn gives another 3 1/2% of the sale price to his agent, that is not different than you giving 100% to the seller and he gives 7% of the sale price to the listing agent, who in turn gives 3 1/2% to the buyer's agent.

DISADVANTAGES OF USING A BUYER'S AGENT

1. In some areas, buyer representation is not a common practice. Only a few agents in your community may practice this. Merely picking an agent because he is willing to represent buyers is not the best way to determine which agent to use. Some agents working for companies who

do not permit their agents to represent buyers may be an agent who will work harder for you to locate the right property. Your primary concern in using an agent is to find an agent who will work the hardest to get you to the right property and the best value. That overrides your decision on who will represent you. However, if you can find an agent who is willing to represent you and will work hard for you, then you've got the ideal situation. Therefore, only work with an agent who will represent you if you also know that that agent will work hard to locate the right home.

2.   When an agent who represents you shows you a property listed by his company, that agent can no longer work solely as your agent. In most instances, he must work as a dual agent representing you and a seller. In such a situation, the agent's fiduciary responsibilities to you will be reduced. He acts as a facilitator in such a transaction. Some real estate companies will not permit their agents to work as a disclosed, dual agent. In such cases, when showing their list of properties, they will require you to use another listing company to see those properties. In my opinion, it is in your best interest to work with an agent who works as a disclosed dual agent in such situations, rather than working with the agent who will not show you properties listed by his company. You may miss out on good deals.

3.   There is no advantage in working with companies whose agents work only with buyers and not sellers. Since disclosure has become common, a lot of companies sprang up across the country who will advertise that they represent buyers only. Is it to your advantage to work with such a firm? There is no advantage in working with such a company in and of itself. Only if that company has the agent you believe who can do the best job in locating you the best property should you consider this.

SUMMARY:
WHY YOU NEED TO USE A REAL ESTATE AGENT

1.   You'll be exposed to more properties. Without an agent, you are limiting yourself to only 10% of the marketplace. 85%-90% of the properties in any given market are handled by real estate agents.

2.   Real estate agents are required by law to present facts to you. They cannot fall through the cracks or change the facts. Homeowners that you deal directly with could be evasive about certain property facts, such as

property values, utilities, zoning, taxes, restrictions, association fees, public transportation, etc. The real estate agent is required by law to present only facts to you. You can rely on the real estate agent because he jeopardizes his license if he is untruthful to you in any factual information.

3. The real estate agent can direct you to the right lender. Just as important as finding a home is obtaining the financing for that property. Lending institutions vary from market to market. Their lending practices are constantly changing. A good real estate agent knows the right lender who can help you get into the property you want. You will never realize your American Dream if you can't get your property financed, unless of course you have cash. Remember when you find your American Dream Home, you want to be able to get it with nothing stopping you. Keep in mind that a real estate agent wants nothing to stop you from getting your home because he receives a commission from the sale! Additionally, a good agent can direct you to a lender who can **pre-approve**, rather than pre-qualify you for a loan before you ever find a house.

4. The real estate agent can answer your questions regarding the purchase agreement, other forms, loan application, processing, settlement documents, various procedures that are confusing to you and may frighten you. Never be ashamed to ask the agent your questions. If the agent can't answer the questions, he has the sources to get the answers. Alternatively, you cannot always rely on what a homeowner says about his property or about various questions that he might not even be aware of. Sometimes, in order to make a sale on the one home that they have, they answer questions in a misleading fashion. Real estate agents can't do that. A good agent will never mislead: he will always get the information and answer your questions properly.

5. The real estate agent can assist you in writing a purchase agreement. Although a real estate agent is not meant to eliminate an attorney, most contracts, if the purchase is on a simplified basis, can be written by a real estate agent. Keep in mind that you must direct him with what to place on the agreement.

6. The agent can act as a liaison between you and the seller. Sometimes it is much easier to communicate with a third party than directly with the seller. You'll find you get more done that way. Real estate agents have a way of communicating with the buyers and sellers to help

make everybody come to an agreement without having emotions get in the way.

7. The agent can monitor your transaction through closing. This includes overseeing any appraisals and inspections. They can keep you informed of any time stipulations and answer any questions up until closing. This is especially crucial if you are buying a home out of state, or far from your present home.

8. The real estate agent's services are free. Remember, it is typically the seller who pays the commission, even if the agent represents the buyer. So why shouldn't you get the use of a real estate agent. It costs you absolutely nothing to do so.

Chapter 8

Your Dream Castle

"A man's home is his castle."

— James Otis (1761)

I'll tell you a real story of a woman who is a real Countess. She lived in a real castle in Europe. She also had a horse farm in Virginia for many years. She decided she wanted to change her life and took a trip destined to California. The plane made a layover stop in Phoenix. She got off, liked the hot climate, got in a cab and asked the cab driver to take her to a nice area. He drove her to Scottsdale. She saw a townhouse that looked nice and immediately called the agent. The agent gladly showed the house to her. The house had a refrigerator with an ice maker and water dispenser in the door and she had never seen such a modern appliance before. She bought the townhouse and of course the refrigerator went with it. She lives happily ever after in Scottsdale, Arizona.

Now, let's look at facts and dream lists that you want in your home.

Dream List

My Dream Castle

WHAT I WANT	Passionately	Would Be Nice	OK/ Not Necessary
Large living room	_____	_____	_____
Great room	_____	_____	_____
Dining room	_____	_____	_____
Family room	_____	_____	_____
Basement	_____	_____	_____
Attic	_____	_____	_____
2-3 car attached garage	_____	_____	_____
Detached garage	_____	_____	_____
Bedrooms (indicate # of)	_____	_____	_____
Porches—any kind	_____	_____	_____
— screened	_____	_____	_____
Large kitchen	_____	_____	_____
Modern appliances	_____	_____	_____
Large closets	_____	_____	_____
Bathrooms (indicate # of)	_____	_____	_____
Fireplace(s) (where?)	_____	_____	_____
Large yard	_____	_____	_____
Small yard	_____	_____	_____
No yard	_____	_____	_____
Swimming pool	_____	_____	_____
Open, airy home	_____	_____	_____
Cozy, closed in home	_____	_____	_____
Lots of trees	_____	_____	_____
Low maintenance yard	_____	_____	_____
Style of Home (write in)	_____	_____	_____
Carpeting (where)	_____	_____	_____
Tile (where)	_____	_____	_____
Heating (kind–write in)	_____	_____	_____
Cooling (kind–write in)	_____	_____	_____
Special features	_____	_____	_____
Other	_____	_____	_____

Chart 8-1 Passion List

This form is available in the Appendix. Make copies and fill out as much as you can every time you think of a passion item. Change and adjust as often as you want.

As you complete this chart, and as you read through this book and answer the questions I have asked you, you are forming in your mind your Dream Castle. It may still be hazy, but slowly it is coming into focus.

I can only give you choices I think of. As many types of people as there are in this world, there are that many choices and combinations in the ideal home. So, I have provided an area at the bottom of this chart 8-1 to let you fill in just what you want.

Next, let's use chart 8-2 to determine the location of your home, taking into consideration your family needs and lifestyle.

Dream List

My Dream Castle Location & Lifestyle

WHAT I WANT	Passionately	Would Be Nice	OK/ Not Necessary
In the country	_____	_____	_____
In a major city	_____	_____	_____
In a small town	_____	_____	_____
Far from major highways	_____	_____	_____
Close to major highways	_____	_____	_____
Close to schools	_____	_____	_____
(what kinds)	_____	_____	_____
Close to a major library	_____	_____	_____
(kind of library)	_____	_____	_____
Close to basic shopping	_____	_____	_____
— food	_____	_____	_____
— clothing	_____	_____	_____
— home repair center	_____	_____	_____
Near entertainment	_____	_____	_____
(list what kind)	_____	_____	_____
How far from work?	_____	_____	_____
(list miles or time)	_____	_____	_____
Horse property	_____	_____	_____
Close to neighbors	_____	_____	_____
(how close?)	_____	_____	_____
Far from neighbors	_____	_____	_____
(how far?)	_____	_____	_____
Near Fitness Club	_____	_____	_____
Near Park & Rec. area	_____	_____	_____
Near Community Center	_____	_____	_____
Has sewage hookup	_____	_____	_____
Has city water	_____	_____	_____
Has city gas	_____	_____	_____
Has city electric	_____	_____	_____
Paved Road to house	_____	_____	_____
Other	_____	_____	_____

Chart 8-2 Location and Lifestyle List

As you complete these charts, and re-work them, your priorities, your passions will become apparent. This will make it easier for you to find the right house.

In finding your Dream Home, here are some things for you to consider:

WOULD YOU BE LIVING IN YOUR HOME A SHORT TIME OR A LONG TIME?

If you are going to stay for a long time, then look at homes that have long-term potential. It will accommodate you and your family for the next 10-20 years.

If you will stay for two to five years, then look for a home with a good resale value. Have it be standard looking, near schools, near other conveniences that would appeal to a general home buyer. Or, it is such a good deal that you can easily fix it and sell it within a few years?

WILL YOU BE RAISING A FAMILY IN YOUR NEW HOME?

Consider the age of your children now, what will be their needs in 5-10 years. Can the house accommodate these needs? Will the neighborhood and location work for you?

DO YOU HAVE A HOME-BASED OFFICE OR BUSINESS?

If you work out of your home, consider what your needs are. A friend of mine started her business in the garage of her newly purchased rural home. The house had one active telephone line. This was used for the home number. She needed one more for the business and another dedicated line for the fax machine. The telephone company charged to put in the second line, which was laid out on the property, but not connected. Then, $400 was charged to lay a third line and connect it. To her, this was worth the effort, but a very expensive way to start the business telephone hookup. The total bill for the connection of all three lines was over $600. Be sure to ask what is available in utilities if you need something specific for your home business or office.

Also, check with the Homeowners' Association rules. Some have strict guidelines as to what sort of business activity you can conduct out of your home. Don't rely on the word of your agent. Have her get the Association's agreements and read them carefully.

HOW FAR DO YOU NEED TO DRIVE FOR YOUR JOB?

Do you need to be near your work? How far is the commute? Will you be driving at peak traffic times of off-time? You may need to fly out of town often. In this case, how is the access to the airport?

IF AND WHEN YOU RUN INTO FOUL WEATHER, WILL YOU BE ABLE TO GET TO THE ESSENTIAL SERVICES?

If you have elderly parents, or small children, consider what your medical needs are. Can you get medical help in an emergency? Similarly, how important are other services to you in case of foul weather? You may be okay if the roads are well paved around you. Or, if you have a 4-wheel drive vehicle. Or, this may not be an issue at all.

HOW MUCH WORK CAN YOU DO YOURSELF ON A HOME?

This is the time to be honest and practical. Just because the nearest home repair center has everything you need, it doesn't mean you can repair everything yourself. Electrical wiring, plumbing, structural changes, take expertise and lots of time. Simple painting and re-finishing is even challenging. Given your work and home schedule, how much can you do yourself?

I know that most people go through homes, listing in rapid succession just what they'll do:

— "Tear this wall down & enlarge the kitchen"

— "Add a counter top & bar area."

— "Put in a tub & a shower."

— "Put in a new lawn & garden."

— "All it needs is new floors, new carpets, paint, and re-finish the doors."

Well, I can go on. Each of these jobs takes considerable work to do right.

So, if you want to fix it, make sure you want to live in a home that is being repaired. Or, fix it, then move in. In this case, be sure you have a place to live while you fix your dream home.

Or consider hiring an expert to fix your home the way you want it to be. If you have been pre-approved, use some of that money as a home improvement loan.

Remember also that you can negotiate with the seller to do a lot of things — like change the carpet, paint, clean the yard, etc. More on this in the negotiation chapter.

WHAT LIFESTYLE DO YOU HAVE & WHAT ARE YOUR PARTICULAR HOME NEEDS?

Here we will talk about the basic & important rooms in your home. They are:

1. **Living area** — What do you need here? Formal or informal? Separated from the house by a wall or part of a great room?

2. **The kitchen** — Do you want a large, roomy kitchen because you need cooking and storage space? Is a walk-in pantry your dream come true (it is for my wife — a must in any house we buy!)? Do you need a sunny & bright kitchen that the whole family can gather in?

I love a large, sunny kitchen that is big enough to have room for a kitchen table and chairs in it. When my wife gets up, she likes to sit in our bright kitchen and enjoy a cheerful, warm area.

You may prefer a smaller kitchen because your activities are not centered there.

3. **The bedrooms** — The Master bedroom, the guest room, the children's rooms, the office — what kind of layouts do you want?

Many new homes place the Master bedroom and bath on one side of the house and the other bedrooms on the other. This is fine if you have an office, guest room, or grown children. If you have little ones, you may need to be closer to your children's rooms.

Also for your bedrooms, consider your sleeping needs. I don't know why, but many homes are built with a huge air-conditioning unit just outside the main bedroom. Or, the pool is just beyond your window and the cleaning motor goes off at 4 a.m.!

Track homes also have air conditioning/heating units just outside the small bedrooms.

In one instance, a friend who lived in California had to endure the neighbor's sprinklers going off at 5 a.m. and the leaf-blowers and lawn mowers starting at 7 a.m. This friend was luckily renting the house. He was a very light sleeper so when he went out looking for a house, he ended up buying a one acre lot, far away from any neighbors, with desert landscaping that required no sprinklers, no lawn mowers, no leaf blowers! Finally, peace.

4. **The bathrooms** — How many bathrooms do you need? Do you need one in your garage for your business? Do you need access to a bathroom from the swimming pool? Do you want a bathtub and a shower in each bathroom or just showers? Do you want separate toilet and shower area? Do you like large roomy bathrooms or small is okay?

Many homes may have a large window on one side of the bathtub. This is fine if you don't need privacy. Also, it is fine as long as it is in a model home and everything looks perfect. What will you need to do to have privacy — window tinting, curtains, blinds, etc.?

5. **The storage area** — Consider the type of garage you need for your car, storage needs, hobbies, tools, etc. Also, if you need a basement. Basements are great places for a teenager with a drum set; washer and dryer; or old furniture for your college kids. Many homes have attics and storage sheds. It is nice to have extra space to grow into and place things for storage.

If there are specific other rooms that you wish to have, add it to your wish list.

WHAT KIND OF YARD DO YOU WANT?

First, consider the size and upkeep. If you just love mowing lawns, and you have an eager teenager who loves to do this on Saturday, then get a house with a large yard with lush grass. You may need to consider lawn/gardening service which can add to your monthly maintenance costs.

Then consider the view from your yard. Nothing like sitting for a barbecue and looking over a junk-yard, or a yard full of old tires and broken cars, or snarly, barking dogs! A nice view, or a nice adjoining property, will increase the value of your home.

Do you need your yard fenced in partially or completely? This depends on your pets & children and the swimming pool.

Consider your children's needs. What sort of yard do they need for play and fun?

Do you want to garden? If so, how and where will you put your garden?

The driveway is important as well. How many cars do you have? Are there restrictions in your neighborhood for parked cars? Can you put your RV on the property? Is the driveway close to the kitchen door for unloading groceries?

WHAT SORT OF UTILITIES DO YOU NEED AND HOW IS THE TEMPERATURE MAINTAINED IN THE HOUSE?

In some areas of the United States, you must have a good central air-conditioning. In other areas, an evaporative cooler works well. In cold weather areas, be sure your heater is efficient & modern. Many of the older homes in the cold weather areas are not well insulated and you can waste a tremendous amount of heat. The same is true in hot weather states. Large windows, huge doors, high ceilings all add to your utility bills. Bear these in mind. You may be able to use attractive window coverings and seal all cracks, and even get better insulation for your home.

WHAT THINGS ARE THERE THAT YOU ABSOLUTELY WILL NOT LIVE IN?

Make your definite reject list: the kind of things that make you say, "ugh," such as

— small claustrophobic rooms

— a bad smell in the house that permeates the whole building

— a house near power transformers or other sound polluters, or microwave towers

— near airports

— next to commercial buildings

— near bad neighborhoods

— near a city dump

— near a cemetery

— near busy streets or highways (find out if your one-lane street will become paved and a major thorough-fare)

— near a railroad track

— a real "fixer upper"

— bug infested, rodent infested home

— a house sharing an access way

HOUSE STYLES

When you are first thinking about what kind of house you want, you probably have a style in mind. Or, you may want a style that is indigenous to your geographical area, such as Cape style; Santa Fe; Ranch style; California style; or whatever.

Here is another friend story: I had a friend who had no idea what kind of a home she wanted. She looked for three years in several cities. She considered an existing home, a new home, a condo, a ranch-style huge home — nothing would really click with her. Finally, she arrived in Phoenix to visit a friend. That same day she arrived, her friend took her to see a home she noticed listed for sale. My friend walked into the empty house and she said: "Wow. There is nothing about this house that I hate." She bought it on the spot. The house is what I call a "plain vanilla" style. But, it suited her needs perfectly and she is very happy with her choice.

The moral of the story is this: unless you have a specific, must-have style in mind, be open. You may find just the right style for you that has all you need.

EXISTING HOMES

An existing home has many advantages, such as:

- established neighborhoods and services

- mature trees and landscaping

- kinks have been worked out

- have personalities in their color, structure, layout, yard areas

- usually more space for your dollar

- have organized, thoughtful things — like a breakfast nook, covered back porch, shelving in a laundry room, area for trash, tool racks, load controller, etc.

- nice landscaping, gardens, fruit trees

Disadvantages of existing homes can be old, leaky plumbing (look for soft floors near the bathtub!); badly wired electrical or low voltage coming into the house; small closets; small windows; dark hallways; cockroaches, etc. Remodeling can easily eliminate many of these problems. If this is the case, be sure to negotiate these changes with your seller.

Also consider the conditions of the outside of the house. If the wood is peeling and chipping, lots of work is needed there. If you need major plumbing in the kitchen or bathroom, you may find crumbling pipes when you open the walls. If you need new caulking, you may have to fix a water-damaged floor or wall.

Inspection of a home is vital. We will cover this in the next chapters.

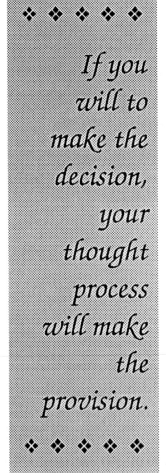

If you will to make the decision, your thought process will make the provision.

NEW HOMES

It sounds great to get a new home. No one lived there before. It is sure to appreciate. Often, you can pick the fixtures and floor coverings before it is completed. Everything is new, so we hope up-to-date, efficient components.

New homes also have advantages and disadvantages. Consider these carefully. Don't think that a new home is trouble-free. Many people get a brand-new home and spend the entire first year calling the various repair people to fix parts of the house. So much can go wrong.

A new home that is a few years old may be a good buy. Many of the problems have been worked out, and everything still new and in good condition.

CONDOMINIUMS AND PLANNED COMMUNITIES

Many people are away on business trips or live alone and need a secure, small home in a planned community. If you are a young working adult, or a retired person, consider the advantages of living in a condo or other form of planned community. You are most likely to be near like-minded people. There are lots of advantages to living in such places.

Although you won't have to do much gardening (or none) or maintenance, these places do have fees to cover these functions.

The advantages outweigh the disadvantages if you measure your needs and this style of home carefully.

Look at the attached tables to help you evaluate your home and your neighborhood. When you find several homes you like, use this checklist to evaluate your potential home.

Dream List

Neighborhood Checklist — Existing Homes

1. What does the home look like overall?

2. In what condition are the neighborhood homes?
   * outside yards, outside paint, parked cars, noise & activity level

3. What sort of noises do you hear?

4. What sort of smells do you smell?

5. What do you see when you look around?

6. How far are schools?

7. How do kids get to school?

8. Do you see graffiti & other signs of gang activity?

9. What are the PTA activities like?

10. Is there public transportation near?

11. Are there good, accessible roads near? What sort of shopping do you have nearby? How far?

12. Is it a safe neighborhood? (watch for bars on windows, gang activity, drug activity, etc.)

13. Are the adjacent neighborhoods consistent with this one? If not, what is the difference? (You do not want a nice neighborhood near a slummy one.)

Chart 8-3 Neighborhood Checklist--Existing Homes

Dream List

Neighborhood Checklist — New Homes

1. What is the builders' reputation (ask neighbors)?

2. Are new homes being constructed around you?

3. Are there amenities nearby?

4. What type of outside finishes and/or yard do you get if any?

5. What are your warranties?

6. Who is your contact person?

7. If something goes wrong in your home, how soon can you expect repair & help?

8. What sorts of other building is going on around you?

Chart 8-4 Neighborhood Checklist--New Homes

Choices, Decisions, Realities. In today's complex world we face the stress of making a number of decisions every day that have serious effects on health and happiness. The choice can often overwhelm us.

Chapter 9

Let's Get Organized

"Stay, stay at home, my heart, and rest; Home-keeping hearts are happiest."

— Longfellow (1897)

It's more fun to sit down than stand up, and I enjoy lying down best. But let's smell the bar-b-que in the back-yard and move on. So let's get off the couch, switch off the T.V. and go house hunting. Join the frantic struggle of Americans trying to get their share of the American Dream. It is tough and difficult to make decisions. I hope my book is helping.

Now let's go over a simple chronology of events that will demystify the process of buying a home. This is based on many years of experience in Real Estate training, personal home buying, and thousands of people with whom I have talked and from whom I have learned a great deal about buyer and seller needs.

When you get up one morning and you decide you want to buy a home, or when you finally come to the conclusion that your present living situation no longer fits your needs, it is time to think of your Dream Home. So, let's do the following:

1. Make a dream list

2. Set your priorities

3. Read this book thoroughly

4. Complete as many tables and charts as you can

5. Clip out photos, articles, magazine ads about homes, furnishings, style of fixtures, color, you name it and paste it up.

6. Make a thorough assessment of your financial condition. Get a credit report, and clean it up if needed.

7. Pay off outstanding bills and get on time with payments if this has been a problem in the past.

8. Find a mortgage lender.

9. Get pre-approved and a letter of commitment.

10. Find a real estate agent.

11. Go over your Dream Castle passion lists and do some soul and mind searching.

12. Find your home

13. Look it over carefully. Consider everything. Does it fit your priorities and your passion lists?

14. Negotiate for what you want. Everything is negotiable, so make sure you attach a separate sheet to your written offer about the conditions of sale, or contingencies.

15. Make a written offer and give a check for "earnest money," or "good faith deposit" ($500 - $1,000 minimum).

16. If you have an opportunity to get your home purchased with seller financing, then look into the financial terms carefully. Have a professional

person — real estate attorney, financial consultant, or the like, look over all papers and agreements.

17. If the seller accepts your offer, you go on; if not, make a counter offer. If you go on, you sign documents to this effect. Or, start looking again. Your home is out there.

18. Escrow is opened by your agent (or you if you are handling the purchase). Total time can take 15 days to 90 days. This is up to you and when you want to take occupancy.

The escrow officer also makes sure all contingencies are carried out, all agreements adhered to, and all conditions are met.

The escrow officer reserves all funds, makes a detailed report of all your expenses, and disburses the funds.

In some states, an attorney handles the escrow functions. Some people like this, some do not. If it is the law, you must have an attorney. Look into the fee structures. If you have a choice, ask your friends and family what are the pros and cons of attorney vs. escrow company, and then make a choice.

19. During escrow, you make sure your home is professionally appraised and inspected. You will need an appraisal and a termite report, as well as have all conditions met.

20. You need to meet your part of the agreement; get the deposit and other financing to escrow by the required date.

21. You do a walk-through the day or two days before you sign the final documents. Word of warning: make **sure** all the commitments, promises, conditions of your agreement are met. **Don't leave anything out.** That last piece of equipment in the yard, the refrigerator to be moved out, may not be done when you are ready to move. Worse yet, the floors, the yard, the walls may be damaged and you have no recourse. A promise to fix a leaky toilet may not be carried out. It is extremely difficult sometimes to get a seller to fix something after he has your money and has signed the final documents.

22. You sign the final papers, get a key and you have your

Dream Home!!!

23. Title is recorded in your name.

24. Complete a Homestead application and mail it in.

PURCHASE AGREEMENT

An offer to purchase a house contains several items. Go over it carefully. I know so much is in small print and boring. Read it, and have it explained if there are unclear parts. Be sure you know and understand everything on this agreement.

If you have added a contingency list on the sales agreement, make sure it is just what you want to say. This is very Important.

I know someone who found just the perfect house — 5 bedrooms, near a business district, close to schools. One problem remained — the wife hated the brown carpet. It had to go or she would not agree to buy the house.

This was clearly stated on the purchase agreement. Ten days of daily negotiating later, the carpet was changed and the deal was closed.

Put everything you want changed, no matter how small or insignificant, in writing. Put on the agreement "see attached addendum" and on a separate sheet, list what you want repaired, changed, or fixed. Mark this sheet: "Addendum to Purchase & Sales Agreement" or "Contingencies for Sales Agreement," and attach it to the agreement.

An agreement consists of the following:

1. Price of house

2. Down payment amount

3. Amount of deposit

4. Terms for financing

5. Who pays for what:

      — street improvements

      — sewer hookup

— other neighborhood charges or bonds

6. Date of occupancy

7. Length of escrow, closing date

8. How will title be arranged

   — tenants in common

   — joint tenancy

   — community property

9. Liquidated damages — meaning that if you defaulted on your agreement, you agree to pay a specific amount in damages to the seller, such as the deposit or part of it. There are laws to govern the amount of charges depending on the State. This it to prevent frivolous Purchase Agreements or frivolous decisions.

   Don't enter into any real estate contract unless you are serious about your decision. You could lose all or part of your deposit. Leave a way out by making a list of "contingency clauses."

10. In case of disputes, how arbitration is handled.

11. What will be left in the house as part of purchase such as:

   — refrigerator?

   — wall air conditioner?

   — satellite dish?

   — pool equipment?

   — washer & dryer?

   — window treatments such as blinds and drapery?

12. If the seller is not a U.S. citizen, does he have tax withholdings?

13. Condition of property

14. Warranties by seller

15. Inspection report

16. Termite report

17. Any tests done on soil

18. Natural hazard area information such as flood zone

19. Zoning changes pending

20. Energy requirements by state if any

21. Home protection plan — for interior appliances, heating, air-conditioning, etc.

22. Home insurance — fire, etc.

23. How and when payments are due

This chapter seems technical and is full of lists. Go over this information carefully so you know what you will be expected to do and what you will sign and when.

Chapter 10

Let's Go House Hunting

"Whoever makes home seem to the young dearer and more happy, is a public benefactor."

— Henry Ward Beecher, *Proverbs From The Plymouth Pulpit* (1887)

Yes, now we are going house hunting. We have taken you through many pages and asked questions and tried to help you make your passion lists and help you realize your priorities.

Now, for the really Big Stuff — **HOUSE HUNTING**

It is only the second day in the job of house hunting, but already we are feeling the pressure. We have to be goal oriented, make sacrifices like getting up in the morning, showering, getting dressed, and out the door and hope today will be better than yesterday.

Finding a home should be lots of fun. I find the better prepared you are, the better the experience.

If you are married and you will make joint decisions, go together if you can. It will save lots of time and wear and tear on you and your agent. If a family member or "significant other" will purchase your home with you, again, if you can, go together. Or, start looking by yourself. Leave family, cousins, and friends out of this process. They will only confuse you. Sometimes even children will confuse you with their enthusiasm for a home that may not be the right thing in many other aspects.

This is a big, important purchase. As much as your family's tastes and preferences are important, do the preliminary looking with as few people as possible.

You can involve your family in the planning and passion lists. Take into consideration what they want & why. Then, you are well prepared for any eventuality. Take into consideration what your family's needs and your work needs will be 5-10 years from now as well.

THE HOUSING MARKET

We are assaulted every day to make decisions, distracted by traffic, everybody wants something: decisions, relationships, marriage, work, Real Estate. When would it be a more convenient time...the next Ice Age? I can't sleep, the Real Estate Agent is calling. HELLO! Time out! The complaints...the ultimatums...the threats...legal action....Tune in yourself. You've got the best idea what you need. Line up your future. New home? Old home? First home? Second home? Bigger? Smaller? Retirement? You've got everything going for you. It's **YOUR** bottom line, **YOUR** dreams.

In the home market, there is what is called a Buyers' Market and a Sellers' Market. A Buyers' Market means there are lots of homes for sale in an area and you can make a good deal with the seller because homes are not selling so quickly. A Sellers' Market is the opposite: less homes for sale; quick sale of existing homes; seller may get pretty much what he asks for. If you are in a Sellers' Market, the more prepared and educated you are about home purchase, the better you will be at finding just what you want and getting it.

Home sales usually peak in the months of May and June. They start off slow in January and drop off again at the end of the year. During the slow months, there will be more homes available on the market and sellers will be more willing to make deals. Be willing to see homes in less than optimum condition considering the cold weather, the bare trees, the dead lawn! However, these are better bargain months.

The peak time of May and June is a good time to move — especially if you have children. But, the seller knows this and it is not the best time to buy. However, we do not always have the luxury of shopping when we can get the best deal.

By now, you have read the chapters about the kind of home you want and where you want to live. You have considered the communities, neighborhoods and all the other aspects of a suitable location.

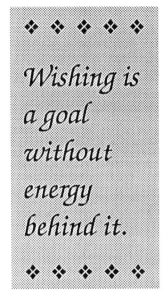

Wishing is a goal without energy behind it.

You may also consider investigating a community regarding future improvements, zoning changes, building plans in the area, and restrictions. Subscribe to a local newspaper (or pick one up for several weeks at the local market), and see what is going on in the area. You can also do your own investigating by asking questions to people you encounter when you shop, eat, get gas, etc. Your sales agent will also be able to get you statistics.

Take out a map of the areas you are considering and study it to see what you are most interested in and how these are connected with the other parts of the city.

As you view homes, ask the homeowners about the neighborhood. Listen carefully to what they say. They will know a lot of things if they have lived there a while.

Business owners, retailers, builders, also will offer you information about the area. Ask about property values, building booms, how fast homes sell in the area, the demand for homes, growth in business and services.

You can also get economic data from government agencies at the Chamber of Commerce. Government agencies dealing with planning, zoning, growth-plans will be able to tell you what are the particulars of an area. Visit a land development firm and find out what projects are in the works for an area.

The Board of Education will give you information on schools and statistics needed for your children

HOW TO FIND HOMES FOR SALE

As I've said before, get a good agent to help you. Refer to previous chapters on how to find a good agent and why you need one.

There are also a number of ways to find homes for sale. Here is a partial listing:

1) Friends, relatives will tell you when they see homes for sale or you can drive around and see where there are For Sale signs. If it sounds good, get the name and number of the listing agent and go and see it. In many areas, there will be an information flyer provided for you under or near the For Sale sign. This will give you the price, and other pertinent data on the house. If you are interested, call the listing agent on the flyer (or sign) and make an appointment to see the house. Often, you cannot see a house without an appointment.

2) Local newspapers and real estate magazines will advertise homes for sale. If you find Open Houses, go and see them. It is a good way to get a view of homes in a neighborhood without committing yourself immediately to an agent.

House ads can sound too good to be true. Or you may find the "perfect deal" that is no deal at all. Stay rational and don't expect everything you see listed to be available nor a true description of what is available.

Here is a list of abbreviations used in listing a home:

ABBREVIATION	WHAT IT MEANS
BA	Bath
BR	Bedroom
MBR	Master Bedroom
LR	Living Room
DR	Dining Room
GR	Great Room
FR	Family Room
CA or C/A	Central Air

2 C GAR	Two-car Garage
BSMT	Basement
FP or FRPLC	Fireplace

You will also run into words used often in the real estate market that mean a motivated seller, such as "reduced," "motivated seller," "must move," etc. Other words that can raise questions, red-flags, or your enthusiasm are: "fixer upper," "handyman special," "needs repairs." However, what is "move-in condition" for a seller may not be your idea of one at all. It's all in the eye of the beholder!

3) MLS Listings are another source for homes. These were discussed in an earlier chapter on Realtors®. There are listings of homes that your Realtor® will get for you, or you can get for a fee. Study these carefully, noting the price, special features, size of lot, directions and more. You may convince your agent to give you the addresses and you can at least drive by and see for yourself.

Typically, an agent will set-up appointments for you and accompany you.

4) Auctions and foreclosures are yet another source for homes. They are sold on an "as-is" basis and can be really good deals.

These homes are advertised in papers. You can also ask lenders for foreclosed properties. County court houses also list foreclosure notices.

Foreclosed and auction properties are being re-possessed by the lender. The owner defaulted on payments and is no longer able to pay. Be sure to follow these guidelines:

— Do a title search — are there back liens or taxes due?

— Have a thorough inspection done. Many homes in this state may not have been maintained.

— Do your homework and know the market value of your prospective home.

— Do not overbid.

— Know the rules of an auction. You may need to make a deposit at the auction or be pre-approved for a loan.

— Know the particulars of the sale — when is it final, what are the contingencies, does the seller need to approve.

Foreclosed properties are also listed in what is called the Resolution Trust Corporation or RTC. This is an agency that auctions properties for the government and they have a list of homes up for auction.

You can call **RTC at 1-800-624-HOME** for a list of properties.

Let me state again: Do your searching and inspecting and know what you are getting into on foreclosures and auctions.

5) You can use your modem and computer to have access to MLS listings if this is provided by the agents in your area. You can even view homes on your home computer without going out and driving around.

You can go to the appendix section and either tear out or copy the pertinent pages that you will need for your home search — the neighborhood checklist, passions lists, home viewing reports — and take these and any other lists you have completed with you. You can make a 3-ring binder notebook and keep all your information in one place — as you start looking and making notes.

SELECTING YOUR DREAM HOME

Unless you are truly well versed in real estate and know all the ins & outs of home buying, go and find a good, professional real estate agent. We have discussed how to find a reputable agent earlier on. A good agent will be able to save you lots of time and irritation.

Give your agent your dream list. Go over your preferences on homes, neighborhoods, styles. Be open frank, and honest. Your agent will respond to you (if he is an experienced professional) according to your communication of your needs. Also, by now you have searched out neighborhoods, have gone to open houses, have had your loan pre-approved, and you are set to go.

Your agent will give you a listing of all homes that fit your description and price range and make appointments to see these homes. Schedule to go out to 2-4 homes minimum and see as many homes as you can in one day. But, don't marathon an 8 hour day! It's too long. You'll be too tired. All homes will start to look the same and you'll get confused.

Take your filed report sheets with you. Use one per home. Attach it to the MLS printout. Write down everything that you feel about the house such as

- Why you like it

- Why you don't like it

- Outstanding features

Complete each filed report as much as possible. Take your time. When you get home, put the rejects in one part of your notebook and the "maybes" in another. You may want to see these again.

Unless you are in a great hurry, take it easy and see as many homes or as few homes that you can handle physically, emotionally, and mentally. don't get overwhelmed, but enjoy the process.

Remember, your Dream Home is out there waiting for you. Go through the process of finding it.

Use the attached list to help you "see" the home properly. Go over this list now. When you go out looking, take this list with you and use it as a reminder. This is not to take the place of a professional inspector — but to serve as a guide for viewing.

Dream List

Viewing Checklist — Outside

1. As you approach the house, what is the road like?
   — easy access, unpaved, paved but bad, other _____

2. What does the outside of the house look like? _____

3. What is the condition of the roof? _____

4. What kind of landscaping? _____

5. What kinds of trees & shrubs? _____

6. If there is a pool, does it look in good condition? _____
   Are there cracks in it? _____
   Is it full of leaves and dirty? _____
   Are there a lot of trees around it? _____

7. Where does the electricity come from into the house? _____

8. What is the source of water _____

9. Is the house on septic? _____
   Sewer connected? _____
   Leach field? _____

10. What is the outside condition of the house:
    paint _____
    windows _____
    doors _____
    gates _____
    porches/enclosures _____
    fences _____
    patios _____
    faucets _____
    — where are they? _____
    — are they leaking? _____
    other structures _____

11. Heating & AC units — What condition are they in? _____

12. Steps — what condition are they in? _____

13. Driveway's condition _____

Chart 10-1 Viewing Checklist--Outside

Dream List

Viewing Checklist — Inside

FLOORS

1. What are the floor coverings and what condition are they in:
   living room _____
   kitchen _____
   dining room _____
   hallways_____
   bathrooms _____
   dining room _____

2. Do the floors creak anywhere?_____

3. Are the floors even? _____

4. Are there broken tiles?_____

5. Is there any evidence of leakage in the bathrooms and/or kitchen? _____

PLUMBING

1. Are there leaking faucets? Check baths & kitchen _____

2. Secure sinks? _____

3. Turn water on to check for pressure _____

4. Leaky toilets? _____

5. Secure toilet bowl? _____

6. What condition are the fixtures in? _____

HEATING & COOLING UNITS

1. Ask how old are the units and what are the repairs made, if any. _____

_____

WATER HEATERS

1. What size is it?_____

2. Does it look rusty?_____

3. Are there signs of leakage? _____

Chart 10-2   Viewing Checklist--Inside

Dream List

Viewing Checklist — Inside

GENERAL

1. What is the total square footage of livable space? _____

2. What are the rooms like?   Large enough?   Closet space?
    Windows?   Placement in house? _____

3. If there is a stairway, is it easy to use for your family? _____

4. Kitchen & Dining areas
    How does it feel to be in it? _____
    Do you like the cabinets? _____
    Do you like the counter space? _____
    Is there a pantry? _____
    Is the kitchen big enough? _____
    Look under the sink, any signs of leaks? _____
    Look in the cabinets, are the shelves straight or warped? _____
    What is the condition of the sink & fixtures. _____
    Does the garbage disposal work? _____
    Does the dishwasher work? _____
    Does the stove & range work? _____

WINDOWS & DOORS & SCREENS

1. Do the doors open easily?
    — Main entry _____
    — Bedrooms _____
    — Bathrooms _____
    — Closets _____
    — Sliding doors _____
    — Sliding screen doors _____

2. Do the windows open and close easily? _____
    — condition of window screens _____
    — condition of sliding door screens _____
    — condition of locks
        — doors _____
        — windows _____

Chart 10-2 Viewing Checklist--Inside p. 2

Dream List

Viewing Checklist — Inside & Outside

LIGHTING & ELECTRICAL

1. Porch lights_____

2. Fixtures in
   - bedrooms _____
   - living room _____
   - dining room _____
   - kitchen _____
   - other _____

3. Are there plenty of outlets?_____

4. Do electrical outlets have enough amps to meet the needs of your
   appliances, computer, etc.? _____

GENERAL

1. Are there any bad smells?_____

2. Does the property drain adequately? _____

3. Where is sunrise & sunset? _____

4. Any particular noises? _____
   - machinery? _____
   - traffic? _____
   - heating, AC? _____
   - neighbors?_____

5. Lastly ask about insulation. What kind of insulation? _____
   Where is the insulation? _____

STORAGE

1. Size of garage_____
   - condition of garage _____

2. Washer/dryer area_____
   - utility sink_____

3. Basement size _____
   - basement condition_____
   - basement access_____

4. Is there an attic? Is it easy to get to? What condition is it in? _____
   - Is there a crawl space under the house? _____

Chart 10-3 Viewing Checklist--Inside & Outside

I know this is a long list, but it gives you an idea so that you are not basing your decision on just feelings. Use your feelings and use facts to decide.

Make copies of these lists and take them along to help you make a proper evaluation of your Dream Home.

Live up or down to your self expectations. Get started...the first home...a launching point to bigger and better.

When you lose the fun of house hunting, get some humor into the process. It's a great weapon.

We now go to decision making.

Chapter 11

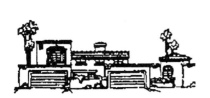

Real Estate — It's a Package Deal

"Home is the place where, when you have to go there, they have to take you in. "

— Robert Frost, North of Boston (1914)

I found the house of my dreams.

You want my money? You get me too — my wants, my wish lists, my dream list. Mr./Mrs. Real Estate Agent, Mr./Ms. Seller, Mr./Ms. Lender.

I sat next to a woman on an airplane flight to Orlando. I was the speaker at a Coldwell Banker Real Estate Convention. The woman had a very large, gorgeous, ten-carat diamond ring. I commented on the beautiful diamond. She said it was the Finkelstein Diamond....That with most large diamonds, it had a curse....I asked, "what's the curse?" She said, "Mr. Finkelstein. It's a package deal...."

Real estate agents will tell you it's a buyer's market or a seller's market. But, it's really your market to make your best deal. Remember, it's your "deal." Whatever makes you happy is the "best deal." You are the most creative, productive, fruitful. It is your home to enjoy, not the real estate agent's. Making a commission is what the agent wants. Is the agent listening to your needs? Has the agent reached his peak performance or has he peaked out? If the agent stopped chasing you, calling you, it is time for another agent. Go back and read the chapters on real estate agents and get fortified.

Most Buyers do not know this, but you can negotiate on everything when you are buying a house. Remember that you have everything on your side: you have been pre-approved, have a letter of pre-approval in the amount of your mortgage, subject to appraisal; you know what you want; now you can get what you want, what you want changed, fixed, moved.

Just what can you negotiate?

- the price of the house

- how it will be financed and terms of financing

- closing costs and who pays for them

- when you want to move in

- outside and inside finishing and painting

- roof repairs, water leak repairs, windows, screens, anything that needs fixing

- clearing and repairing yard & landscaping

- what fixtures remain or get changed

- window treatments: blinds, drapes

- pet houses, pet doors

- washer/dryer

- furniture

- refrigerator

- patio furniture

- potted plants

- satellite dish

- bird bath

- will you be credited for prepaid taxes & insurance

- carpets & flooring

- dishwasher

- anything you consider you want or do not want

You can ask for anything you want. As far as I'm concerned, all a seller can do is say "no."

The most important negotiating points are the price and terms. You can get a house as low as 6% to 25% or maybe more below the asking price if you know how.

Don't rely on your agent to help you set the price. Some are good at this, some don't want to go down in price — especially if he is working for the seller. It is up to you to figure out what your offer will be. You can always go back & forth. Also, don't let anyone talk you into a rush-decision, such as: "there are lots of people interested, so you must decide quickly!"

I know of many instances that this is not the case. Even if someone else gets in ahead of you, believe me, you will still find your Dream Home.

Don't succumb to pressure or fear or even being placed in an embarrassing position. When you feel pressured, don't decide. When you decide, you should feel happy & elated.

If the market is hot & homes are moving fast, then you need to be prepared to make quick decisions. If the market is slow, then you can hold out for what you want. Always shoot for the best deal; the price **YOU** want, the terms and conditions **YOU** want.

If you have decided to negotiate directly with the seller, then you will do this face-to-face. Otherwise, your offer will go on a written agreement and be presented to the seller by your agent.

There is nothing embarrassing at all in making a low offer, asking for the drapes, change of carpets, the refrigerator, and the fancy lights in the dining room. Don't let your agent's reluctance worry you. It is the agent's job to present any offer you are willing to make with whatever conditions you attach.

LOOKING AT A HOME

Go to the homes you have listed in the MLS Printout (or whatever listing you have made). Take along your helpful charts which you have placed in your notebook.

You will look at homes first as an overall impression:

1. Is it in my price range?

2. Is it what I want?

3. How do I feel about it?

If you look at, say, six houses in one day, you will have a clear idea of the "Definite Yes," "Definite No," and "Maybe" categories.

Write on each MLS listing & attach it to any comments you have. Use the Viewing Checklist forms in the Appendix for each house. Put all the "No's" in one part. Save these so you can appreciate the work you are doing. The "Maybes" go in a separate section, as do the "Definite Yeses."

Try to narrow down the field. Go back and see the homes, and eliminate more as you go along. Focus on a location in which you are interested. Finding a home can take a few days or as long as you want it to take. You can get tired, frustrated, and irritated. It all depends on how much you are motivated to decide and move. If you have two weeks to find a home, move, get to your new job, and put the kids in school, your decision-making process is speeded up. If you've already sold your home and you must move, you are likely to decide faster.

There is right timing in everything. Just as you found your first car, your spouse, your job, your home also will be found — all in good time.

When you find a home, or houses you like, look them over in a leisurely manner. Get a good "feel" for the house. If you like it enough to come back, say so, make an appointment, and return with the other decision makers in your family.

View the home you like in daytime, and for lighting and neighborhood at night. Check out the various parts of it using the chart in the Appendix as a guideline. Inspect it as much as it is feasible for you to do so.

Although you will want and need a professional inspection to look at your prospective home, if you know a good handyman, take him along and have him make a general inspection.

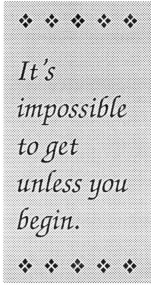

It's impossible to get unless you begin.

Ask the owner why the house is on the market. Try to find the motive of the seller to sell the home. This will give you clues as to how much motivation there is to sell and accept an offer.

A typical buyer may look at 20 homes or more before making a decision. So, stay organized and keep all your notes in the proper places.

As you tour the house, ask whatever questions pop into your head. Carry your notebook and make notes as you go along. Ask your agent or the seller about absolutely anything that comes up. Remember, it's your money. The answer must satisfy you.

As you look at homes, remember there will be several that will fit the bill. A friend of mine and his wife found a house of their dreams in a small town. They returned to Chicago after making an offer. The offer fell through. They remembered another home they liked but barely remembered all the details. They called their agent and made an offer. The offer was accepted and they moved 60 days later. They told me later that there were specifics they could not remember, and thought they were settling for second best. After they moved, they realized how nice the house was and were very happy in their choice, and really got the best choice after all.

Ask yourself if the house has everything you want. Use the checklist. Imagine yourself living in it. Just stand quietly in the various rooms and look around. How does it feel for you? Can you overlook the dark cabinets and gold shag carpet? Can you imagine yourself using all the various rooms and enjoying it?

Walk through carefully. Open doors, cabinets. Look at toilets, showers, bathtubs. Press on the floors. Look at the ceiling for evidence of leaks or termites. Termites leave tell-tale brown spots or long brown spindly looking threads. Open windows, sliding doors. Look in the closets and cabinets.

Go outside and walk the property. Ask questions. Smell the air — is there an odor? Are there things you like or dislike?

Will your furniture fit in this house? Does the water taste good? Is the shower fixture too low?

Finally, what things do you dislike that can be changed? It is important to keep a perspective on this. For a price, anything can be changed. You can't have the house moved, so the only thing you can't change is the location. Ask yourself if you really want to make all the changes.

How much change are you willing to make? How much can you spend on re-decorating? Finally, how much can you have the seller do to make the deal?

Carpeting, flooring, paint, window treatment & windows all can be changed with ease. Will the seller put new carpeting in to make the deal? Faucets, kitchen & bath remodeling, add-in windows, doors, need more professional work and more money.

More serious work such as new landscaping, putting in a new roof, new sprinkler system, is even more costly. Consider changes carefully.

When you decide you like a house, you can start the negotiating process. Your offer can be made contingent on inspection. If you can have a professional inspector do a careful check of the home before the offer, do so. If not, you will make your offer based on the inspection report.

If you think you will do major re-modeling or repairs, get an estimate by a licensed contractor.

Go into the negotiations feeling armed with what you want and what needs to be done.

Before you make an offer, do the following:

- Use your checklist to evaluate the condition of the house.

- Go around the neighborhood and find out if it is acceptable.

- Find out what are the applicable taxes for the house. Will the taxes go up? When is the home going to be re-assessed — when sold, or in a few years?

- Go over any chart you want to check the house with. Ask any question that comes to mind.

Remember: get the seller to do all you want if you don't have extra money for changes.

Chapter 12

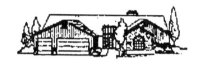

Get The Best Deal

"Money is time. With money I buy for cheerful use the hours which otherwise would not in any sense be mine."

— George Gissing (1903)

You have found your home. Now you need to make an offer and negotiate what you want.

THE OFFER PROCESS

When you decide you love a home after making all your compromises, working your dream lists, found the best home that fits your need in the price range you can afford, you now make an offer to the seller. The offer is written on a pre-printed form. Specific components of a form may vary in different regions of the United States. However, the following is usually included:

1. Descriptions of property & address

2. Names of agents involved

3. Financial information: total price, down payment, amount of deposit, price you will offer.

4. A time limit for response from the seller, for getting inspection, getting repairs, meeting all your needs, closing the deal.

5. A list of conditions you want met. Be sure you go over this carefully. Put your requirements on another sheet of paper if you want. Call it "Addendum to Purchase Agreement."

6. Add that you expect your full deposit be returned if your requirements are not met.

SAMPLE CONTINGENCY LIST

This agreement is contingent on the following at the seller's expense (add this to the sales agreement):

1. The leak in the master bathroom faucet is fixed.

2. The ceiling rain damage is repaired.

3. The washer and dryer be part of the offer price.

4. The flower pots remain.

5. The brown carpet be changed.

6. The wallpaper in the kitchen removed and walls painted.

7. The crack in the swimming pool needs to be repaired.

8. The bathroom leak is repaired.

9. The cut trees and garbage cleared from the yard.

10. All furniture removed completely before the walk-through date.

11. The landscaping maintained until closing of escrow.

12. The insurance, home maintenance contracts all maintained until closing.

Remember, you can ask for whatever you want as a condition for sale. If it is important to you, stick to it, if not, then see what you will back off from and what you must have. We call these unimportant requests "throw aways." We always add a couple of "throw aways" to the negotiation list.

Always start the offer with a lower price than you will settle for. If you want the seller to do major repairs, then ask for them. If you will do the repairs, deduct them from your offer.

Put **everything** in writing. Make sure you are serious about everything you really want. Once an offer is accepted, it is a legal document.

HOW MUCH TO OFFER

Ask your agent to get you a list of sales prices of comparable homes in the neighborhood. This will give you an idea of the value of the house. Sometimes, you need to consider what you are getting in size, quantity, age of home, remodeling, etc. that may be cause for higher or lower prices.

The best deal is the least expensive home in the best neighborhood.

Most homes sell for about 6% less than their list price. This is an average. The real figure will depend on many factors concerning the house, the market, the change in neighborhood. How badly the seller wants to sell now and what a cash buyer is worth to him.

You can also have the selling price subject to an appraisal. If the appraisal is lower, you can offer the lower price. Consult the mortgage company or lender on an appraisal value.

There was a home offered for sale for $125,000. It was a custom home in which the builder-owner still lived. He was a good builder and loved his home. A market survey showed comparable homes in the area sold for under $100,000. An offer was made for $120,000. It was flatly rejected. A second offer came for $98,000 by another buyer immediately after the first offer was rejected due to being unsure of qualifying for a mortgage. The first buyer backed off. The seller accepted the second, cash offer. The sale closed in 15 days!

The moral of this true story? Neighborhood prices don't always tell you the whole story. Things change. There is always someone who wants a house badly enough to pay the asking price.

I feel that if you want to bargain, be flexible. If your seller is motivated, he is more likely to deal. If not, and if there is a deep pride of ownership, then the seller will not be as flexible.

To get a feel for the seller's mood, consider the following:

— How long has the house been on the market?

— Has the price been reduced?

— Can you find out what the original purchase price was?

— What is the remaining balance on the loan?

— Do the sellers have another home and they have to move?

— Have there been other offers?

— Is the couple divorcing?

Rely on yourself to make your offer. You have looked around, you know what you can afford, you know how much you want the house, you be the judge.

The seller will not accept anything less than what is owed on the house. Any new decorations, features, up-dated remodeling must be considered. But, don't buy an over-priced, over-built home.

You must stay with the agent who showed you the property and not try to circumvent his commission. So, be fair and don't try to make an outside deal. You can do this only when the listing date has expired. Then you can deal directly with the seller or hire a new agent.

An appraiser will also help you determine the market price. Use this as a guideline for your offer.

WHAT ARE THE TERMS

Carefully consider what terms you want met before you will close the deal. Include this in your offer. Put down in writing what you want from the seller:

- what specific repairs

- what timing you need for repairs, occupancy, inspection, etc.

- what condition must the house be in — everything removed, yard clean, etc. Be specific.

- check on taxes, maintenance service, insurance, warranties, Homeowners' Association fees.

- will the seller pay for some or all closing costs? Ask the seller to pay for appraisal, inspection, title search, etc.

- will the seller fix the sprinklers? do the painting on the porch? replace flooring?

CONTINGENCY CLAUSES

A contingency clause gives you a way out if the house does not ultimately meet all your needs. Common contingencies include the following:

— termite inspection

— selling of your own home

— getting the job transfer

— satisfactory home inspection report and who pays for it

— is the seller required to repair, clear out infestation, if inspection shows problems?

— other inspection reports such as for radon gas, asbestos, lead paint, rodents

— house appraisal — which has to be done for complete approval of your loan amount for the house. State what you will do if the appraisal is lower than the selling price.

— pending price your contractor will charge for remodeling, major repairs, etc.

— set time limits for response offer

Don't be frivolous. Be fair and honest. If a seller wants to counter your contingencies by wanting to continue showing the house, he can do so. This is called "kickout" clause. You then can decide to back out or remove the contingency clause.

Get a time limit within which a written response is received — usually 24-48 hours. You can cancel an offer anytime before it has been accepted.

In the past, people found homes and then needed 30-60 days to get a loan and get all the paperwork done before they could move in.

Now, when you are pre-approved, you can go through the process quickly. It will all depend on what contingencies you have placed and how long it will take to meet them.

You want to make sure the sellers are completely out, and everything is totally to your stated and agreed upon terms before you sign the final papers. If the seller will remain after the closing, put the terms of the agreement in writing.

Especially state what property attached or non-attached stays in the house.

In addition, state what condition of cleanliness you want the house to be left in. Put in the offer that you want a walk-through. This is important so that you can check the property when it is empty and that all the requirements are met.

Handle all prorations in your negotiations. If taxes, insurance, landscaping fees have been paid up beyond the closing date, are the sellers entitled a refund or is this part of the deal?

Make sure your agent goes over any other provision you will need. For example, ask what kind of fire damage insurance the house has during the selling period.

YOUR DEPOSIT

When you make a written offer, a good faith deposit (earnest money) is usually made. This check is held in escrow and you are entitled to its return if the offer is rejected, or you reject the counter-offer.

Make sure the terms of the refund are spelled out clearly. Most sellers have no problem with refunds. Spell out how and when you expect your refund. Usually, your check is not cashed until the escrow process starts after all parties agree on the offer.

Offer as little a deposit as you can. No need to tie-up your money. If you really want the house and it is a hot market, offer a larger deposit to show your serious commitment.

Once your offer is accepted, you may put an additional deposit. Any deposit you make is usually figured in as part of your total down-payment. You will see the entire balance sheet at the close of escrow.

Don't give the deposit to the seller. It must be held in escrow until closing of the purchase. The deposit can be held by the agent as well, but in a separate trust account — one that is not commingled with the agent's account.

An escrow company is a neutral third party and the best place to hold deposits. All parties involved in the transaction have to abide by the escrow rules. If there is a problem, both parties have to wait until a judgment order is made in court and instructions given to the escrow officer.

- If the seller does not accept your offer, you get your deposit back.

- If your contingencies are not met, you get your deposit back.

- If your set contingencies include your down payment being gifted, your job being transferred, and these do not occur, you get your deposit back.

- Spell out everything in your offer agreement.

You already have your pre-approval letter, so you don't have to worry about financing unless better terms are available concerning this purchase, such as a low interest assumable, an assumable FHA or VA loan, or an attractive owner financing that beats your loan.

When you decide to make the offer, explain to your agent exactly what you want to do. Have him put everything in writing. Sign it, attach your deposit, and let your agent present it.

Your agent will present your offer to the seller and seller's agent face-to-face, phoned or faxed. Your agent can make a tremendous difference here by the way he presents your offer.

Within the stated time period, the seller will either accept, reject, or make a counter-offer in writing.

- If your offer was accepted, you start the purchase process.

- If your offer was rejected, make another offer if you are still interested.

- If a counter offer was made, then go over it carefully and decide what to do next. You have to respond within a set time limit as well.

The seller can counter with anything he wants — the price, the contingencies, etc. He will address his counter to any or all the items you listed.

Whenever you or the seller accept an offer or counter offer, the purchase process starts.

If you counter again, make the desired changes, re-state your position, have it presented in writing once again.

This can go back and forth until one party backs out or accepts.

Stay within your passion lists, your priorities, your determination — but also be flexible. It is a fine balance to know when to accept, when to reject.

Don't create a bad feeling with the seller by being ugly. If you can't accept his offer, back off graciously. There are other houses around.

If the seller is desperate, and it is a buyers' market, you can make a low offer and it may be accepted. Your agent is required to take **any** offer to the seller — regardless of how he feels about it. But don't offer so little that you can lose a house you really want.

If you are anxious, this is what you want, give it your best shot and tell the agent this is it. The seller may accept.

You have no negotiating power if other offers are coming in for the same house. You have to accept the consequences or make another offer.

So, before you make an offer, consider all the particulars: the seller's anxiety, the market, your passions, your budget, your timetable. Leave room to negotiate.

YOUR OFFER IS ACCEPTED — NOW WHAT?

Once the buyer and seller accept the terms, you are party to a legal agreement. You cannot back out now without legal ramifications.

Are you happy?

Are you scared?

Are you asking yourself "what was I thinking?"

Relax. This is normal. Making a large commitment is filled with anxiety unless you are a pro.

Go back and think of the original reason why you wanted to buy a house. Also, why you love this house, and why you want this house. Sometimes all the right reasons seem far away and less important.

Imagine your new home. Imagine your new neighborhood. You can actually visualize daily being in your new home. This helps you make an easier emotional move.

Get a copy of your signed agreement. If you want, have an attorney look it over. If this is important to you, don't sign until you have it professionally reviewed. Make sure your attorney is a specialist in real estate.

Now start making appointments for the home inspection, termite report, and other specifics in your contract. You may have only 15 days to satisfy these

If you keep doing what you've been doing you'll keep getting what you've been getting.

requirements. Often, your agent will get the appointments made for you and see to it that all the required inspections are met.

Call your local water, gas, electric companies and ask if they do any free inspections of their respective utility lines and outlets. Some areas in the country have this service and you will find these inspectors very well trained and well suited to inspect equipment and connections that are up to code or not code. They look for trouble spots and let you know.

A roofer, air-conditioning expert, termite inspector, and other experts are worth the peace of mind.

If you are having remodeling done, you can have a contractor look at the house and give you an idea of cost, time needed, and other possible needs.

In the meantime, the escrow process begins. We will deal with this process in the next chapters.

WHEN CAN YOU WITHDRAW AN OFFER?

You can withdraw your offer to buy a house without legal problems under the following circumstances:

- before the seller has signed and accepted

- anytime you do not accept a counter offer

- any time the contingencies agreed upon are not met — such as problems found by the inspector

Neither you nor the seller can back out of a signed agreement. You may lose your deposit and be sued. You can sue the seller if he withdraws.

Don't deceive yourself, we are the only ones who can choose truth over deception. The roof doesn't leak! The collapsed ceilings over the closet is because I didn't clean the leaves out of the rain gutters. The roof does leak. Check everything out yourself on your Dream List. Put your doubts into the Purchase Agreement. Make it right. You have to eat a lot of broccoli before you can get that hot fudge sundae.

Chapter 13

Your Home Inspection

"The house praises the carpenter."

— Emerson (1836)

Let us talk about your home inspection, because this is a step you need to take usually within the first 15 days of having your offer accepted or accepting a counter offer.

It is absolutely essential that you have a professional inspector look at your house.

Your agent can recommend an inspector or you can find one listed in the yellow pages. Or call ASHI (American Society of Home Inspectors) and ask for a referral — see appendix for the number. I know a great contractor who also does home inspections. He is so meticulous and fair that you will know what is visibly wrong with your house after he is done looking. He will also tell you about the soundness of the structure, how long you have until your heating and AC units will give out, whether or not your water heater is up to code, and other potential problems.

Most inspectors will look to see if everything is in operating condition. In my experience, they do not look for previous trouble spots that may have been covered over.

A friend of mine moved into a newly purchased home. The cabinets under the sinks in the bathrooms and kitchen had new floor boards. They looked nice. Within a few weeks, my friend noticed a leak under each sink! The leaks were not detected by an inspector and the owner never fixed them — just covered them up.

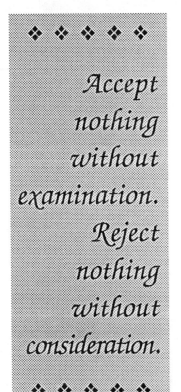

Accept nothing without examination. Reject nothing without consideration.

A good inspector will look for trouble spots and let you know. You can also go over what you want and make clear how you want the home to be inspected.

Depending on the law in your particular area, it is required that a seller disclose any defect on the property that affects the value of your home. You can ask the seller to disclose defects even if this is not a requirement.

You should **still** get an inspection. If and when you still want to proceed, you can negotiate with the seller: have everything fixed, or drop the price to cover the repairs. Of course, you have already made your offer contingent on the inspection report.

If the inspection report shows problems you would rather not deal with, you can withdraw your offer.

Ask the inspector what sort of training he has. Is he certified. You can call NIBI — the National Institute of Building Inspectors, and find out if the person is certified.

The cost for inspection is about $200 - $400, or more if you want other tests done, such as radon, water, etc.

The inspector visually checks the house and evaluates the condition of the house and property. Then, he gives a written report.

It may take at least two hours or more for an inspection. If you are able to, go with him. Ask questions & evaluate.

Dream List

Inspector Checklist

Here is a minimum number of things an inspector should check:

- Attic
- Basement
- Ceiling, walls, floors
- Door, windows, screens
- Foundation
- Electrical system
- Heating & cooling systems
- Insulation
- Ventilation
- Sewer lines
- Septic
- Wells
- Exterior Walls, decks, porches
- Property — drainage, fences, paved areas
- Garage
- Plumbing

The inspector is checking for the following:

1. Cracks & separation
2. Proper functioning of doors, windows, faucets, electrical outlets, etc.
3. Proper drainage of gutters
4. Proper drainage of sinks
5. Signs of leaks
6. Safety & proper electrical wiring
7. Condition of furnace & AC unit. If you live in hot climates, you may want a separate AC man to check the condition of the heating/cooling units.
8. Need for painting
9. Leakage in basement, attic, ceiling — look for water damage
10. Test to see the type & depth of insulation

Chart 13-1 Inspector Checklist

You and your lender also want a termite inspection. The seller usually pays for the termite inspection. Check to see when the last termite treatment was. If you live in a termite problem area, be sure you continue the termite protection plan. This gives you an annual termite inspection & treatment of infested areas for a low annual price.

If you want water, radon, sewage system inspections, you will need separate inspectors for these — unless your home inspector is qualified to do them.

An inspector is a generalist. He is looking for obvious problems. You will need a specialist if there is any particular type of inspection you want or need.

The inspector also does not deal with carpets, wall coverings, color, or any other cosmetic issues. Nor does he tell you the value of the house.

The inspector should not offer to repair the house, nor refer you to one. He should not give advice on purchasing the house.

THE INSPECTION REPORT

When you get an inspection report, you will see just what was done and the condition of each area. The report will also indicate the weather condition or anything else that may have conditioned his inspection.

See the attached report — you will note how the categories are broken down and how each is evaluated.

Decide what areas that need fixing you can ignore (light bulbs); what areas you want fixed by the seller; what areas you can handle yourself. Decide how this will be handled financially: you pay or seller pays? Then re-submit your offer. You can withdraw your offer if the report is not satisfactory to you.

Generally, you can negotiate to repair, change, fix anything. It is all up to you. Mostly, sellers will repair things that affect living conditions — leaks, broken doors & windows, malfunctioning units & components, etc. If you want anything changed, you must indicate this.

My suggestion is that you must know in advance what are the likely repair costs. Be prepared so you are not putting undue pressure on yourself and your finances.

Chapter 14

Why Insurance?

"It is extraordinary how many emotional storms one may weather in safety if one is ballasted with ever so little gold."

— William McFee (1916)

Yes, you need the basic *Homeowners' Insurance* against damage caused by fire, theft, & other hazards and against personal liability. This protects you if someone is injured on your property. All lenders require this. If you live in flood areas, or earthquake areas, you may also need insurance for such damage.

There is also *Homeowners' Protection Plan* insurance which covers your possessions, heating and AC units, kitchen appliances, plumbing, garage door openers, fans, electrical in the house and more. You can buy additional coverage depending on what you want insured.

Some lenders will also want you to buy *Mortgage Insurance*. This protects the lender in case you default, or are unable to pay for a period of time.

Title Insurance is also required by lenders. This protects your ownership should any problems arise.

When you are ready to buy insurance, make sure you compare several companies. You will be surprised how different the monthly payments are. Get at least 3-4 quotes. When you are in the middle of making an offer, it is sometimes difficult to think of one more item to shop for. But, it will save you money.

Also, check with the owner to see if the home has any warranties or protection plans that you may want to continue, such as termite inspection plans. See when these plans expire and decide if you want to continue coverage. Shop around for these as well and get the best price for your coverage.

BASIC COVERAGE

Your basic homeowners' insurance covers your property.

The cost for your insurance varies depending on how comprehensive is your coverage, how much the house is covered for. Once you get the basic coverage for fire, theft, and other perils, look at the policy carefully to see if you want more coverage.

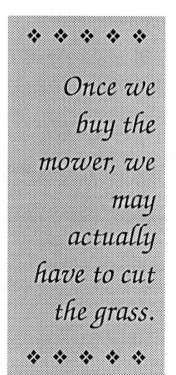

Once we buy the mower, we may actually have to cut the grass.

Your lender will require at minimum the purchase price of your house less land value. You may want additional coverage for replacement value of your home & personal property.

The replacement value of your home (the structure) is the total square footage of your home multiplied times the cost per square foot. A local builder or contractor can estimate the cost per square foot.

The replacement value of your possessions can be calculated by taking inventory. You may have limits for some items, after which you will have to pay more.

When you purchase significant items, or make major improvements, be sure to update your coverage. If you have computer equipment, or an office at home, make sure these items are covered. Save receipts for all major purchases. Don't scrimp on insurance. Get an adequate policy. If you want to pay less, you can increase your deductible.

Some insurance companies offer discounts for multiple accounts (home & auto). Also, a burglar alarm and smoke alarms (you should have smoke alarms in your home) will reduce the cost of coverage. Coverage may be slightly higher in rural areas or hazard prone areas — since fire trucks & emergency vehicles will have to travel farther to get there.

Find out clearly what is covered & not covered, especially for roof damage, water damage, etc. When you purchase your home, you will be required to pay, up front, for a one year policy. Find out what the deadline is for this from the escrow company. Your insurance company gives you a paid receipt, or your escrow company adds this to your closing costs: you pay the entire closing cost to the escrow company & they disburse the funds.

If your lender will allow, you can purchase home insurance that is paid on increments throughout the year. The insurance company relays the information to your escrow company.

MORTGAGE INSURANCE

If you have a down payment of 20% or less or an FHA loan, your lender will require mortgage insurance.

For FHA loans, you need a mortgage insurance called *mortgage insurance premium* or MIP. Conventional loans require insurance called *private mortgage insurance* (PMI) if your down payment is less than 20%.

You pay an FHA loan mortgage insurance at closing of escrow at the rate of 3% of the loan amount, plus a monthly fee.

If you sell your home or refinance your FHA loan, you may be entitled to a refund.

For private mortgage insurance, your method of payment and monthly charges will vary. You may pay a higher first year rate than later. This is added to the monthly payments of your mortgage.

If and when you reach a certain amount of equity (20% at least) you may be able to cancel the private mortgage insurance.

The lender will require a written notice, may also require an appraisal, and have other requirements before you can cancel, such as a clean payment record on owner occupied property.

TITLE INSURANCE

Title insurance is required on all homes. It is purchased when you close. It insures that no one can claim ownership of the house but you.

The lender insists on a title search to make sure no one else will lay claim — after all, the lender is really like a partner with you. Usually, the escrow company does the title search tracing the history of the ownership of the house. The search involves looking at all records pertaining to the owners of the house — deaths, divorces, judgments, taxes, wills, etc.

You will need to know that the home is free of unpaid taxes, liens, assessments, or an easement against it. For example, an *easement* gives another party — public or private — the right to use your property to access a driveway, put up utilities, etc. *Encroachment* means that the boundaries of your property are clearly marked & no structure of yours or your neighbor's crosses over the boundary lines.

If any unclear title to the property appears, it has to be completely cleared before you have title.

As much as a title search is supposed to uncover and clear problems, it is not a *guarantee* that nothing will happen to challenge your ownership. A lender requires insurance therefore, to protect itself against any losses if there is a challenge. You can purchase a lender's title policy (covers lender) and, or, purchase an owner's title policy (which protects you).

Usually, the cost of title insurance is a one-time payment. You and the seller may share the cost. The insurance is good as long as you own the house.

Shop around for title insurance. Find out what kind of insurance is required by your lender.

A LAST WORD ON INSURANCE

If you are going to conduct business out of your house, or will be having any expensive equipment such as computers and printers, inquire about coverage. You may need to pay a little extra for liability and possessions, but it is worth your while to do so.

Chapter 15

What Are My Total Costs?

"To make a happy fire-side clime. To weans and wife. That's the true pathos and sublime of human life."

— Robert Burns (1789)

At this point, you are aware that buying a home costs you more than the purchase price of the home. We have gone over the specific items you will need. In this chapter, we will combine all the information on costs regarding the purchase of your home and present this to you in an organized fashion.

Here is a list of expenses that are included in closing the escrow. Your particular home, the lender you have chosen, the method of payment, what the seller will contribute, will alter some of these costs. This is a general list. Go over it, discuss it with your agent, lender, seller, and the escrow company. Negotiate.

Many of the costs we have spoken about, such as insurance and inspection can be paid before closing. Or, if you agree, all moneys due can be given to the escrow company in one lump sum and disbursed to all claimants.

CLOSING COSTS

1. *Down payment* — the amount of money you will put on the house — money that you saved or received as a gift. Your earnest money should be applied to this total.

2. *Mortgage* — the total asset of the loan that the lender gave you to purchase the house.

3. *Loan application fee* that you may have paid up-front when you applied for the loan.

4. *Points* are one-percentage point each that some lenders require you to pay. Two points are two percent of the total loan amount. This is tax deductible in the year paid (check with your tax accountant before you decide on the lender).

5. Loan origination fee is usually one percent of the total loan amount. It is not tax deductible.

6. If you assume a mortgage, you may have to pay an *assumption fee.*

7. You may also have to pay for the *credit report* when you apply for your loan. Or, it may be part of the application fee.

8. *Appraisal fee* is paid when you make your loan application.

9. A *home inspection* is paid by you (sometimes a broker pays for this, or the seller) when the inspection is done. You may be able to give the escrow company all moneys due & they disburse the funds. The same for any other sort of inspection.

10. *Processing fees* are sometimes charged by the lender for the loan.

11. *Interest may be prepaid* on your loan for the month.

12. You pay *mortgage insurance* if it is required by your lender.

13. You pay for *home insurance* for one year (or however arranged) when you are closing.

14. *Property taxes*, if due when you purchase the house, must be paid for. The seller may also have paid for the full year and will be reimbursed, unless you negotiate otherwise.

15. *Settlement fee* may be charged by a settlement company.

16. If you have a *real estate attorney*, you pay his fees.

17. *Title search & title insurance* may be paid by you, the seller, or combination of both.

18. *Recording charges* are due for recording the deed & mortgage.

19. Some areas assess *transfer taxes* for county, city, state.

20. If the lender requires a *survey*, you will need to pay for this service.

21. You will need to pay *homeowners' association* fees, if applicable.

22. The *deposit* you made when you first made the offer. Put as small deposit as possible. Try $500 or $1,000.

Your taxes and insurance are usually calculated as part of your monthly mortgage payment. However, if you borrowed money privately, or financed the home in another way other than a standard loan, you will have to arrange tax & insurance payments on your own.

Your escrow company will tell you what are the total charges and itemize the entire bill. Review this carefully. Before the closing date, you will have to bring a cashier's check or certified check for whatever balance you owe.

Use the chart attached to figure out your closing costs.

Dream List

CLOSING COSTS

1. Deposit (earnest money) $ _____
2. Down payment   _____
3. Mortgage — monthly payment   _____
4. Loan application fee   _____
5. Points — total amount   _____
6. Loan origination fee   _____
7. Assumption fee   _____
8. Credit report fee   _____
9. Appraisal fee   _____
10. Home inspection (if you have one) _____
11. Processing fees   _____
12. Interest — prepaid   _____
13. Mortgage insurance   _____
14. Home insurance   _____
15. Property taxes   _____
16. Settlement fee   _____
17. Attorney fees   _____
18. Title search   _____
19. Title insurance   _____
20. Recording charge   _____
21. Transfer taxes   _____
22. Survey fees   _____
23. Homeowners' association fees   _____
24. Other   _____
25. Total closing costs $ _____

Chart 15-1 Closing Costs

After you close, file *homestead papers*. You get these forms from your agent. There is a small fee for this. This insures you that should there be a lawsuit filed against you, your home is safe from being taken from you. Do this as soon as possible after you move in.

Your house payment is made *in arrears*. This means your October payment is made in November. When you close, you have to pay whatever mortgage is due for the remainder of the month you are in.

All closing fees are negotiable. Typically, the fees mentioned are paid for by the buyer. But, you can negotiate to have the seller pay for some or most of them. For example, you have to purchase a basic homeowners' insurance policy. However, you may be able to negotiate with the seller or the agent to pay for the home warranty policy.

When you first shop for a mortgage loan, look for lenders who do not charge *points*, or very low points. Ask lenders what other charges you will have to pay. You may be able to find a lender who charges very little or no processing fees, points, or document preparation fees. Know in advance of your decision to go with a lender. However, the riskier is your credit history, the less choice you may have. Lenders in the business of high risk mortgage loans have loans with higher interest rates and may have additional charges tagged on.

Other loan charges may include an "account set-up fee," charged to you to arrange for your payback! Or, it may include "tax service fee," charged by the lender to set up the payment of your tax & insurance moneys — they hold the moneys and pay out at appropriate times. These should also be a part of the lender's services offered.

I have recommended to you that you get your pre-approval loan first, **before** you go looking for a house. Now you can see why: you have cash from which to negotiate with the seller and you are not distracted by the wear & tear of house hunting and can shop around for the best loan package.

You are a customer. **Lenders** have to serve you. So, ask up front; know **exactly** what is required from you regarding your loan.

You should not be paying for the lender's or seller's attorney fees for **anything**. You will have to pay your own attorney's fees if you hire one. If you have an attorney, discuss *in advance* what those fees are: Are they hourly? One lump sum? Some states do not have attorneys involved unless there is a specific need for one.

When it comes to recording fees, they should not exceed $7-$12 per document. Ask for an explanation if it is more.

Escrow companies charge for their independent work and set up title search, complete all closing transactions, hold all deposits and moneys, and disburse all funds, as well as record documents. This is a flat fee. You may split these costs with the seller. Or, you can ask the seller to pay for these fees.

Any other charges during the close of escrow should be clearly marked — and your part of the payment clearly indicated.

Be sure you are paying **only** your part of the taxes, interest, insurance, etc. You should not pay for anything unless that payment is for the exact time you take possession of the property.

Title insurance is a must for every house purchase. However, title companies vary in their charges. Find one that is cheaper at the time escrow is opened. Shop around. The seller pays for the standard title insurance, the buyer for the additional title insurance. Be sure you do not pay for both.

HOLDING TITLE

Holding title means the proper name on the purchase of the home — the owner. There are several kinds:

1. *Sole ownership* where you are the sole owner.

2. *Tenancy by the entirety* for married couples only. When one dies, the ownership goes to the other spouse without legal proceedings.

3. *Joint tenancy* is used when two or more people are the owners. Any one owner can sell his interest in the house without needing approval from the others. When one owner dies, the surviving owner gets the share of the one who died.

4. *Tenancy in common* means one or more owner; when one dies, his part goes to his (the deceased's) heirs.

BEFORE CLOSING & WALK-THROUGH

I can't emphasize enough the importance of this. Of course you remembered that when you made your offer, you were specific, among other things, on the following:

1. Contingencies

2. What goes & what stays

3. Date of occupancy

4. Condition at close of escrow & final walk-through

5. You want a walk-through before signing all papers.

Before you sign any final papers, go to the home and walk through it. Use your checklist attached to your agreement. Make **sure**:

1. Everyone has moved out

2. All items to be removed are removed

3. All items to remain are there

4. No new scratches, scrapes, holes, or other damage was incurred while moving

5. All repairs have been done as promised.

If anything is not according to your stipulations, you can open the transaction for renegotiation.

Check all major systems to be sure all are in working order. Check the appearance of the house. Are all personal properties removed? Are the agreed upon items there? Have any fixed properties (hardware, carpeting, stove, etc.) been removed?

If the seller was to remain after closing and pay rent, then you have arranged for this. Otherwise, the seller, or renter, or any other, must be out of there.

When the final walk-through is approved, you are ready to close.

Make sure you have all the moneys due at this time in the form of a cashier's check.

Go to the escrow company (or attorney if it is being handled by one) and review **all** documents. Be sure all is in order.

Your lender has already given you a full disclosure of your loan requirements, fees, payments, interest rates. You have your promissory note to pay the lender. You know the date and amount to be paid and other loan information (where to send payment, penalties, etc.).

The lender holds the deed of trust, which restates the information on your loan note.

You may have to sign affidavits as to use and occupancy of your home.

You will receive the deed — signed by the seller — stating the property is being turned over to you. This is recorded at the registry of deeds. You may be asked to sign IRS forms.

Your lender will give you a disclosure statement if he intends to sell your loan to a secondary market.

If any error is made, you agree to re-sign the agreements. You also sign a document stating you are still employed, are 18 years or older, are sane, etc.

You will sign lots of documents, pay the balance of what you owe. The escrow company disburses the funds and sends you a disbursement statement. It states who pays for what, the closing costs, the selling costs. If you paid fees before closing (POC — paid outside closing) this is noted. You get a sort of balance sheet.

You Now Get the Keys. You Are the Owner of a Home!

LAST MINUTE HITCHES

You may run into last minute problems. Stay relaxed. Don't blow up & do "I told you so's." Don't make everyone miserable just because you are overwhelmed.

Stay calm. Stay happy. Resolve problems instead of making them larger than they are.

What to do in case of problems? Let's look at some:

1. During your walk-through, something was not done. If it is minor, ignore it. If it is large, and you did not know about it, you must take action. Don't close escrow until all is completed. A word of warning: Don't agree to a closing date without stating that **all** contingencies must be first met.

2. You should have no last minute money disputes or hidden charges. Get all your finances cleared first and this will not be a problem — get pre-approved. Shop around for a lender who does not charge for all kinds of ridiculous things.

3. If a title problem comes up, clear it before signing.

4. Any other problems, you can take to arbitration. Be fair and ethical. The home will not look the same as it did when it was occupied. It is now up to you to make it fit your needs and your personality.

Here is a pre-closing checklist (see attached checklist as well):

1. Contact all utility companies & have all utilities hooked up & transferred to your name. You can do this by telephone.

2. Arrange when will you do the final walk-through — time and date.

3. Collect all documents you need to bring to closing.

Dream List

PRE-CLOSING CHECKLIST

1. Final walk-through Date and time: _____

   — all things operational? _____

   — all items to be removed done? _____

   — all agreed on items in place? _____

2. Utilities

   — gas _____

   — electric _____

   — telephone _____

   — water _____

   — other services (garbage, etc.) _____

3. What documents do I need? _____

4. Total $ amount I need for closing _____

5. Time, place, date of closing _____

Chart 15-2 Pre-Closing Checklist

Dream List

CLOSING CHECKLIST

1. Hire an attorney, if necessary. _____

2. Make final financial arrangements. _____

3. Insure the mortgage, if appropriate. _____

4. Arrange for homeowners' insurance. _____

5. Get other needed insurance. _____

6. Have property surveyed and appraised.
   (If you go through a lending institution for a
   mortgage, it should handle these details.) _____

7. Arrange for general building inspection. _____

8. Arrange for specific inspections as needed. _____

   — roof _____

   — ac/heater _____

   — utilities _____

9. Arrange for termite inspection _____

10. Do final walk-through. _____

11. Ask about warranty deal. _____

12. Know your closing costs. _____

13. Have cashier's check prepared for closing. _____

14. Have the deed recorded after closing. _____

15. Other _____

Chart 15-3 Closing Checklist

Dream List

CLOSING COSTS CHECKLIST

Initial Mortgage Payment $ _____

Loan Origination Fee (charged by the lender)   _____

Loan Discount Fee (points charged by the lender)   _____

Loan Assumption Fee (if applicable)   _____

Prepaid Mortgage Insurance (if required)   _____

Credit Report cost   _____

Property Survey   _____

Inspections of Property cost   _____

Recording Deed   _____

Prepaid Homeowner's Insurance for First Year   _____

Prorated Property Taxes for Current Year   _____

Attorney's Fees   _____

Closing Company's Fees   _____

Title Search and Insurance (usually paid by seller)   _____

Credit Life Insurance   _____

Down Payment (earnest money)   _____

Balance Earnest Money Paid   _____

Other   _____

Total $ _____

Chart 15-4 Closing Costs Checklist

Chapter 16

Moving Hints

"Peace is a daily, a weekly, a monthly process, gradually changing opinions, slowly eroding old barriers, quietly building new structures."

— J.F. Kennedy (1963)

Moving in can be fun. Moving away from friends and relatives and schools can be upsetting.

Now sit down and visualize yourself in your new home. See how nice it feels, how much you will enjoy it, the garden, the kitchen, the living room. Go over mentally all the little things you loved about it when you first saw it.

Do this often until you actually move in.

Have a garage sale and clear out all your unwanted stuff.

Save packing materials. You can purchase additional boxes and return unused ones.

If you can afford it, hire a moving company. You may be surprised to see how favorable a moving company's costs are compared to your labor, truck rental, equipment rental. Shop around and get quotes.

Do any painting, cleaning of your new home **before** moving in.

Fill out change of address cards and give to the post office. Have flyers made of your new address with a nice note about your move and mail it to your friends.

Meet your new neighbors. Start putting in flowers in the garden and put beautiful things in your new home.

Keep all your new home documents, warranties, receipts in a *new house* file.

If you can, start moving a few personal items slowly, putting something away every day. I have a friend who takes a potted plant, food, and her clothes first thing into a new home. She makes it look nice immediately.

Mark all the boxes with the contents and room descriptions. Put in piles in the garage. Take to the proper room only those boxes you will unpack and put away. This way, you will not be overwhelmed with a truckload of boxes you step over for three weeks (or more!).

On moving day, have a few boxes packed with essentials: soap, towels, bedding, clothes, food items, disposable utensils, baby bottles and baby food, toys, etc.

Treat yourself to a nice dinner out, a hot bath, & go to bed early. Get rest, tomorrow you will start unpacking.

Dream List

MOVING DAY CHECKLIST — PART I

1. Boxes — size & # needed: _____

_____

2. Mover's name: (or attach card)_____

Mover's address: _____

Mover's contact person & phone: _____

Estimated cost of moving: _____

3. If doing it yourself, Truck Co. Name: _____

address, tel #: _____

estimated cost of truck rental: _____

equipment needed: _____

blankets needed (for moving):_____

other items needed for packing the truck:_____

Total cost: _____

4. Who will help to move us?_____

_____

5. Time & place to meet:_____

6. Packing tape: (several rolls & min. 2 dispensers) _____

7. Marking pens (3 minimum):_____

8. When movers will arrive at new home: _____

9. Who will meet the movers: _____

10. What I need with me at the house first:_____

_____

11. What my children will need (food, toys, baby-sitter?):_____

_____

Chart 16-1 Moving Day Checklist--Part I

Dream List

MOVING CHECKLIST PART II

12. Change of address to post office: _____

13. Utilities

    gas: _____

    electric: _____

    water: _____

    garbage pickup: _____

    telephone: _____

14. Send "we've moved" cards to friends: _____

    (check off names in your telephone book as you send them)_____

15. Things I need to do to new home before I move:_____

    _____

    _____

    _____

    _____

16. Things I need to do to old home before I move:_____

    _____

    _____

    _____

    _____

17. Other: _____

    _____

    _____

    _____

Chart 16-2 Moving Checklist--Part II

There are companies that aid you with handling the details of moving-related paperwork. With one phone call, supplying them with information about your credit accounts & addresses, magazine subscriptions, frequent flyer accounts, etc., they inform all your "accounts" of your new address & phone number. They will even change your phone service for you — anywhere in the country. All this for a small fee. I know several people who have used this service and said it cut their moving stress in half — all for about $35!

He's intercepted the ball at the 45 yard line. He's broken away, down to the goal line for a touch-down. He's really earned his 12.5 million today.

Glossary

Adjustable Rate Mortgage: ("ARM") A type of loan where the monthly interest rate can go up or down, usually within established maximum limits.

Agent: A person authorized to work on another person's behalf.

Alienation: Any process where the title is transferred from one owner to another owner/entity. This can be voluntary or involuntary.

All Inclusive Trust Deed: (Sometimes called a "Wrap" or "Wraparound" Mortgage) — A mortgage which is junior in time to one or more earlier mortgages. These earlier obligations become a part of the new mortgage.

Amortization: The process of paying off the loan balance in specific, certain, and usually equal periodic payments. An amortization table shows the declining balance.

Annual Percentage Rate: The true rate of interest for your loan. It includes any points paid, mortgage insurance, etc.

Appraisal: An estimate of the value of a property.

Appreciation: The increase in value of a property over time.

Asking Price What the seller is asking for his property. Consider it an "opening bid."

Assessed Valuation: The amount your property is valued for tax purposes.

Assignment: Term used to describe a transfer of an interest or estate in real or personal property.

Assumption: (assumable) A purchase of property where the buyer agrees to take over the seller's loan.

Backup Offer: An offer which is left "on the table" to be considered if a prior pending offer is rejected by the Seller.

Balloon Mortgage/Payment: A payment which is usually larger than the periodic (monthly) payment. It comes due after a specified period of time. The monthly payments are amortized over the 15 or 30 year loan period, but the loan is actually due in a shorter time such as 5, 7, or 15 years.

Base and Meridian Lines: survey lines which describe a property location in terms of the compass headings of North, South, etc.

Basic Policy: A basic homeowner's insurance policy. Read the form for specific items covered and not covered.

Basis: The value of your home for tax purposes.

Bid: The amount that is offered by the buyer.

Book Value: The value of a property on a financial statement. Involves acquisition cost, plus improvements, less depreciation.

Broker: A person authorized to open and run a real estate agency.

Bundle Of Rights: The privilege of Enjoyment, Use, and Disposition of real or personal property.

Buy Down: Situation where developer or seller arranges for the buyer to get a loan at less than prevailing market rates. This may be done by the developer or seller paying the interest costs to lower the interest rate, but usually raises the price of the house.

Buyer's Market: A period of time when there appears to be an oversupply of real estate inventory and a buyer can usually get a better deal.

Cap: The limit placed upon an adjustable-rate mortgage. The maximum interest rate for the loan.

Cash Flow: A person's spendable income anticipated for each (usually monthly) period.

Chain Of Title: The documented history of recorded documents which report all transfers, conveyances, loans and other charges secured by or impacting upon the subject property.

Clear Title: The ownership (title) is not tainted, clouded, or encumbered by any liens, judgments, claims or other defects.

Closing: Term for the final procedures in a real estate transaction including the signing of all required papers and the recording of the title transfer and the disbursement of escrow funds.

Closing Costs: Buyer and Seller each receive a settlement sheet detailing expenses and credits incidental to the sale and purchase of the property. This will include down payment made by buyer and the real estate commissions, title policy, etc.

Closing Statement: This is a written itemized statement which accounts for all receipts and all disbursements relating to the real estate transaction, including any items which were completed "outside of escrow."

Cloud on the Title: A lien, encumbrance or any other legal proceeding which appears to challenge the owner's ownership of the property.

Commitment: A written contract to provide funding. To be enforceable it should contain the amount and the terms from the lender.

Compound Interest: The required payment of interest on the principal plus any accumulated interest.

Comprehensive: An expensive type of homeowners's insurance that covers most types of damages.

Contingency: A provision in a contract that said contract will be valid when an act or acts have been completed. This could be, for example, the additional signature of your spouse, inspection reports, sale of your property, etc.

Contract: An agreement between parties which is based upon one party accepting the offer of the other party and the transfer of valuable consideration. Frequently described as offer and acceptance.

Conventional Loan or Mortgage: A loan made by a financial institution but not guaranteed by any federal government entity.

Credit Report: A report on all debts which a person has accumulated. This usually involves retail expenditures but could also reveal private loans on real estate, delinquent taxes and legal matters such as judgments or orders.

Covenant: An agreement, usually in writing.

Debt Service: The amount of money which is required to make the payments which the lender has scheduled to amortize the loan.

Deed: [Quitclaim] A document which shows who owns the property.

Deed In Lieu Of Foreclosure: Giving up title of property to avoid foreclosure.

Deed Of Trust: This is becoming the most common method of providing security to the lender. A third party Trustee, quite often a title company, holds the actual title (deed) to the property. When the note is paid in full the title is conveyed to the buyer (borrower).

Default: Failure in making payments as agreed to.

Description: Legal method of giving the exact dimensions of a property.

Discount: To sell for less than the "face" or market value.

Earnest Money: Payment or deposit accompanying an offer to purchase.

Easement: A right to use someone else's property or land for a particular purpose such as access.

Effective Age: The age of a property as estimated by its condition, wear and tear, and past use. This takes into consideration reconditioning or remodeling.

Egress: A right to exit from your property by crossing another property.

Encroachment: Anything that extends over the property line and on to the property of another.

Encumbrance: A claim against or attached to a property (for example a recorded lien, easement or judgment).

Equity: The market value of a property after subtracting all encumbrances.

Escalator Clause: The provision in most adjustable rate mortgages which allows the lender to make changes in the amount of payment required based upon periodic adjustment of the rate of interest. In effect, the escalator provision allows the interest, therefore the payments, to go up and down.

Escrow: A third party is selected to hold items of value for delivery to the parties upon completion of transaction.

Estate: The measure or extent of the legal interest an individual has in real property.

Failure Of Consideration: Not providing value, such as giving someone a "bad check."

Fannie Mae: The Federal National Mortgage Association.

Freddie Mac: The Federal Home Loan Mortgage Corporation.

FHA: Federal Housing Administration

FISBO: For Sale By Owner.

Fixture: Personal property that is permanently attached.

Forbearance: Not taking legal action in a situation where a default has occurred.

Force Majeure: an event that cannot be anticipated or controlled. In real estate, commonly an unavoidable delay in performance due to circumstances beyond the control of any party.

Grace Period: Time between when a payment is due and the date the borrower is assessed late charges.

Grantor: The seller named in a deed or the party conveying a property.

Guaranteed Mortgage: A mortgage that is guaranteed against default such as a loan made by the FHA or VA. The lender is insured against loss by the government.

Home Inspection: An inspection performed on your home by an experienced individual familiar with construction and maintenance of real estate.

Housing Ratio: The percentage of your housing payment (principal, interest, taxes, and insurance) to your monthly gross income. Lenders will use this ratio to qualify you for a loan. Sometimes this ratio is called the front ratio. A common ratio is 28%.

Impound Account: (or escrow account) An account where funds are held by the lender to pay future charges against the property such as taxes and insurance. Also where sums for other closing obligations are kept.

Index: An economic table or indicator used to set the rate for an adjustable rate mortgage.

Joint Tenancy: Equal and undivided ownership in a property by two or more individuals.

Lien: A claim against a property.

Loan Origination Fee: A fee charged by the lender.

Lock In: A guaranty of a certain interest rate for a definite period of time.

Loan To Value: (LTV) The amount of the home price that you have financed.

Market Value: The price at which a property can realistically be sold. Sometimes called "current value."

Maturity: Time when a loan or note is due and payable in full.

Mechanic's Lien: Placed against a property by a contractor or material supplier to insure that their product or services on the property are paid.

Mortgage: A written contract or document between the lender and the borrower where the real estate is given as security for repayment of the loan.

Mortgagee: The lender.

Mortgagor: The borrower.

Multiple Listing: A listing service (sometimes called MLS) which provides members information on real property by classifications such as location, type, price, and specific features.

Negative Amortization: When the monthly loan payment does not cover the principal or interest. The balance on the loan increases.

Negotiation: An alternative to litigation. People meet and discuss how to resolve their differences so that an agreement can be achieved.

Non-Assumption Clause: A provision in a mortgage or loan stating that the entire loan is due upon a sale and cannot be assumed.

No-Recourse Clause: A clause in a purchase offer or a loan stating that the mortgaged property is the sole collateral and source of payment for the loan.

Offer: A written instrument signed by the buyer containing terms of purchase at a specific price and under a specific set of terms. Only when an offer has been accepted, in writing by the seller do we have a "contract."

Opinion Of Title: The legal opinion which is provided by a title company or attorney about the condition of the title to a property.

Option: A written document providing the buyer the right to purchase a property at a certain price, during a specific period of time and under terms such as described above under "Offer."

Original Cost: Includes the amount of cash, the mortgage loan, commissions and services, labor, and materials which were assembled in order to acquire the property.

Originate: To gather all information and process a loan.

Origination Fee: A charge by the mortgage lender for processing the paperwork on a loan application.

Package Mortgage: A mortgage that has personal property pledged in addition to the real property.

Passing Title: Giving title to another party. This may be by gift, sale or by devise (will).

Personal Property: Any property which is not real property or affixed to property such as a radio, furniture, stereo, an automobile or clothing.

PITI: Principal, Interest, Taxes, and Insurance, which is the total monthly payments you make on your home.

Point: A point is the same as one per cent of the total that is charged by a lender to give you a loan.

Prime Rate: The rate charged by a lending institution on short term loans to their best customers.

Prorate: Proportional division of fees - such as taxes, so that they are paid according to closing date.

Punch List: Usually before close, but after an inspection, the items which must be corrected prior to passing title.

Qualifying: The process of determining that a purchaser is financially fit to obtain funds to purchase the desired real estate and make the periodic payments on the debt created.

Rate: The annual percentage rate of your loan expressed numerically. For example, a thirty year loan at a fixed rate of nine (9%) per cent.

Real Estate: Includes the actual land (soil or rock) and everything built on it, attached to it with the intention of being a permanent part of the property (a fence is a good example), and anything growing on the land.

Re conveyance: The legal process of transferring the title to property back to a prior owner.

Refinancing: The act of obtaining a new loan and paying off the existing loan.

Regulation Z: One of the provisions of the federal government's "truth in lending" rules. It is intended to make you aware of the actual cost of the money you borrow.

Rescind: A legal right to withdraw from a contract. This may be based upon misrepresentation, inability to make necessary improvements, or under the terms of Regulation Z (three day cooling off period).

Residential: An area designated for single family homes. Can include apartment buildings.

Rider: An attachment to a contract. Very common in the insurance industry. Make sure you read each one.

Right-Of-Way: The easement that has been granted to allow crossing over another person's property.

Simple Interest: Interest which is computed upon the loan principal amount only. "No interest on accumulated interest."

Special Assessment: An unplanned charge for a condition or need that is placed against all property owners in a defined area to pay for a necessary public improvement or repair project.

Standby Fee: A fee which the lender requires in order to issue a written commitment. Usually this is non-refundable if the loan request is not processed within a given period of time.

Standby Loan: similar to above, this is a commitment to loan for a fixed time and at a fixed amount. A fee is charged for this, and the purchaser can close on the loan if the rate remains attractive or allow the commitment to lapse as better rates and terms are available elsewhere.

Statute Of Frauds: In some states a fundamental part of the State Constitution and in all States a doctrine of the law of contracts that all real estate contracts must be in writing and signed to be enforceable.

Tenant In Common: Typically used by two or more persons who each own equal shares of the property. If one person dies that share goes to his or her estate.

Time-Is-Of-The-Essence Clause: This is put in a contract to insure that the time schedule is adhered to and that no "grace period" exists relative to dates such as "close of escrow."

Title Company: A private company that prepares reports on the condition of title and usually provides an insurance policy against defects in title.

Underwriter: The lending institution that approves (underwrites) a loan.

Unencumbered: A property that is free and clear.

Useful Life: A term found frequently in appraisals. It is the period of time that a property may be considered functional and thus useful.

Variance: A permission from a government agency to allow an exception to a zoning ordinance or building code.

Waiver: The voluntary surrender or abandonment of a right, title, claim or privilege.

Without Recourse: The creditor must look to the security only and cannot collect from the obligor's other assets.

Wraparound Mortgage: See All Inclusive Trust Deed.

Zoning: The rules that establish how a property may be used.

Home Buying Who's Who

Attorney

Name:_____

Address:_____

Telephone:_____

FAX: _____

Beeper:_____

Escrow Company

Name:_____

Contact Person: _____

Address _____

Telephone:_____

FAX: _____

Beeper number:_____

Homestead Office

Address:_____

Telephone:_____

Insurance Company — Home Protection

Contact person: _____

Address:_____

Telephone number: _____

Fax:_____

Insurance Company — Homeowner

Name of Co. _____

Contact person: _____

Address: _____

Telephone number: _____

FAX: _____

Mortgage Lender

Name of Co. _____

Contact person: _____

Address: _____

Telephone number: _____

FAX number: _____

Property Appraising Company

Name of Co: _____

Contact person: _____

Address: _____

Telephone:_____

Fax: _____

Property Inspection Company

Name of Co: _____

Contact person: _____

Address: _____

Telephone:_____

FAX: _____

Real Estate Company

Name of Co.

Name of agent: _____

Address: _____

Telephone: _____

FAX: _____

Beeper: _____

Termite Inspection Company

Name of Co._____

Inspector's name: _____

Address: _____

Telephone: _____

FAX:_____

Title Company

Name of Co:_____

Contact Person: _____

Address: _____

Telephone: _____

FAX: _____

Utilities Inspector

Inspector:_____

Telephone: _____

Others

(Complete form or attach business cards for each category.)

Resources

Appraisers

1. American Society of Appraisers (referral for appraisers)
   800-272-8258
2. Appraisers Association of America
   212-867-9775

Credit Reports

1. Equifax
   P.O. Box 740241
   Atlanta, GA 30374
   800-685-1111
2. TRW
   P.O. Box 2350
   Chatsworth, CA 91313
   800-392-1122

Home Loans

1. Fannie Mae (Information on home buying)
   Customer Education
   3900 Wisconsin Avenue NW
   Washington, DC 20016
2. Farmers Home Administration (FmHA information)
   U.S. Department of Agriculture
   Washington, DC 20250
3. Federal Housing Administration (FHA information)
   Washington, DC 20410
4. Veteran's Administration (VA loans)
   810 Vermont Avenue NW
   Washington, DC 20420
5. U.S. Department of Housing and Urban Development (Discrimination complaints)
   Fair Housing Division
   451 7th Street SW
   Washington, DC 20410
   800-669-9777

Housing Information

1. Fair Housing Information Clearinghouse
   P.O. Box 6091
   Rockville, MD 20850
   800-343-3442
2. Home Buyers Warranty
   Customer Service
   HBW
   1400 Montreal Rd
   Suite 240
   Tucker, GA 30084
3. Home Owners Warranty
   P.O. Box 152087
   Irving, TX 75015
4. National Institute of Building Inspectors
   424 Vosseller Avenue
   Bound Brook, NJ 08805
5. TransUnion
   P.O. Box 7000
   North Olmstead, OH 44070
   312-408-1050

Dream List

Your Family Makeup And Inside Livable Space				
ITEM	NUMBER	KIND / SIZE	YES	NO
Number of adults				
Number of children (now or future)				
Number of retired who will live with you				
Pets — cat, dog, birds, other				
Number of bedrooms				
Living room				
Family room				
Home office/library				
Game room, hobby room				
Workout room				
Kitchen — small, medium, large?				
Dining room — formal? informal?				
Bathrooms — half, 3/4, full size				
Windows in bathrooms?				
Basement				
Garage — 1 car, 2 car, 3 car?				
Windows in garage?				
outside door beside garage doors				
attached or detached?				
Heating — heat pump, natural gas, electric, radiant, solar, coal				
Air Conditioning				
Evaporative Cooler				

Dream List

Your Family Size & Style/Outside Spaces			
ITEM	KIND / SIZE	YES	NO
What kind of garden space do I want?			
What kind of front yard do I want?			
What kind of back yard do I want?			
Do I want a swimming pool?			
Barbecue			
Patio — covered or enclosed?			
Fenced yard			
Total privacy			
Other			

What other front and back yard qualities do I most want?

Dream List

Neighborhood			
ITEM	TOP PRIORITY	MED. PRIORITY	NO PRIORITY
Condition of other houses			
Friendliness of neighbors			
Good schools			
Strict Homeowners' Association Rules			
Proximity of:			
grocery store			
specialty foods			
schools			
libraries			
colleges			
clothing stores			
parks & recreational facilities			
my neighbors			
medical care			
emergency care			
gas lines			
high power electric lines			
radio towers			
sewer hook-ups			

Dream List

ITEM	YOU	SPOUSE/PARTNER
Car Payment		
Personal Loan Payment		
Student Loans		
Credit Cards Total Payments		
Insurance — auto		
Insurance — life		
Insurance — medical		
Property Payments		
Other		
Total (each column)		
Grand Total (both columns)		

Your Monthly Expenses

Dream List

ITEM	YOU	SPOUSE/PARTNER
Gross Salary		
Bonuses, commission		
Interest Income		
Dividends		
Social Security		
Pension funds		
Alimony		
Child Support		
Other		
Total (each column)		
Grand Total (both columns)		

Your Total Income

Dream List

Name		As of	
Description	Market Value	Financing	Cash Value
Cash on Hand			
Checking Account			
Savings Account			
Certificate of Deposit			
U.S. Government Bonds			
Corporate/Other Bonds			
Investment in Business			
Partnership			
Cash Value Life Insurance			
Cash Value Retirement			
Cash Value Profit Sharing			
IRA			
Trust Fund			
Personal Loans Owed You			
Automobile(s) Value			
Recreational Vehicle			
Jewelry			
Collections			
Art			
Furniture			
Appliances			
Computers			
Cash			
Other Assets			
Total Cash Value			
Total Available Cash			
Total Cash Gifts			
Borrowed Money (conventional loans)			
Borrowed Money (relatives)			
Total Cash Available			

Personal Asset Data Sheet

Dream List

QUESTIONS TO ASK YOUR LENDER

1. What types of loans are offered?

2. What is the current interest rate?

3. How many points do you charge?

4. What are the application fees?

5. Do I need mortgage insurance?

6. Can you lock in the rates?

7. Can a loan be prepaid without penalty?

8. What are the escrow requirements?

9. What is the fee for late payment?

10. Do I have a personal contact when I have questions?

11. Who will be my contact person?

Remember: Keep calling your contact person to push for your **Pre-Approval letter.** Find out if they need more information or additional questions answered.

Dream List

AGENT QUESTIONS

1. What is the firm's reputation?

2. What is the agent's specialty?

3. How long has the agent lived and worked in the area?

4. Is the support staff friendly?

5. Does the agent return your calls promptly?

6. Does the agent have a calm and friendly personality?

7. Does the agent seem like he knows his business?

8. Can you see the agent's resume?

9. How many properties has he listed this past year?

10. How many sold?

11. Does your agent take time with you or is he in a hurry?

12. Is your agent organized?

13. Does your agent listen to you?

14. Do the houses you look at match what you told the agent?

15. Does your agent show you houses listed mostly with his firm?

16. What real estate courses has the agent taken lately?

Dream List

QUESTIONS TO ASK YOUR AGENT

1. How much will I pay you for your services?

2. What services do I pay for?

3. Do you require a retainer?

4. Who pays the commission? Seller? Buyer?

5. What are the terms of the exclusivity agreement?

6. What kinds of services can I expect from you?

There are many things you need to know from your agent. Sometimes, the seller may reduce the price of the house to cover his commission. Or, the seller may pay the commission. What we want here is to help you buy your Dream House spending as little of your money as possible.

Dream List

AGENT CHECKLIST

Here is a checklist for choosing the right agent. The agent you select should score the highest. But if the agent does not score at least 10 points, keep looking.

1. Good experience with agent in past sale or purchase. (5 points)_____

2. Agent is highly recommended by someone I trust.   (5 points)_____

3. The company which the agent works for is highly recommended by someone I trust.   (2 points)_____

4. Agrees to work as the Buyer's Agent.   (5 points)_____

5. Got recommendation from lender or title company.   (2 points)_____

6. Agent has closed 25 transactions within the last year.
                                                          (5 points)_____

7. The agent is new but is aggressive, knowledgeable, well dressed, communicates well, shows desire to work extra hard and on weekends.
                                                          (5 points)_____

8. Says to you "Let me know if you see something you like and I'll help you."   (–5 points)_____

9. Willing to show you FISBO's.   (3 points)_____

10. After interviewing three, your "gut" tells you this agent is the right one.   (3 points)_____

11. Agrees to fulfill all your reasonable requirements.   (3 points)_____

                                                  Total_____

Dream List

My Dream Castle

WHAT I WANT	Passionately	Would Be Nice	OK/ Not Necessary
Large living room	_____	_____	_____
Great room	_____	_____	_____
Dining room	_____	_____	_____
Family room	_____	_____	_____
Basement	_____	_____	_____
Attic	_____	_____	_____
2-3 car attached garage	_____	_____	_____
Detached garage	_____	_____	_____
Bedrooms (indicate # of)	_____	_____	_____
Porches—any kind	_____	_____	_____
— screened	_____	_____	_____
Large kitchen	_____	_____	_____
Modern appliances	_____	_____	_____
Large closets	_____	_____	_____
Bathrooms (indicate # of)	_____	_____	_____
Fireplace(s) (where?)	_____	_____	_____
Large yard	_____	_____	_____
Small yard	_____	_____	_____
No yard	_____	_____	_____
Swimming pool	_____	_____	_____
Open, airy home	_____	_____	_____
Cozy, closed in home	_____	_____	_____
Lots of trees	_____	_____	_____
Low maintenance yard	_____	_____	_____
Style of Home (write in)	_____	_____	_____
Carpeting (where)	_____	_____	_____
Tile (where)	_____	_____	_____
Heating (kind—write in)	_____	_____	_____
Cooling (kind—write in)	_____	_____	_____
Special features	_____	_____	_____
Other	_____	_____	_____

Dream List

My Dream Castle Location & Lifestyle

WHAT I WANT	Passionately	Would Be Nice	OK/ Not Necessary
In the country	_____	_____	_____
In a major city	_____	_____	_____
In a small town	_____	_____	_____
Far from major highways	_____	_____	_____
Close to major highways	_____	_____	_____
Close to schools	_____	_____	_____
(what kinds)	_____	_____	_____
Close to a major library	_____	_____	_____
(kind of library)	_____	_____	_____
Close to basic shopping	_____	_____	_____
— food	_____	_____	_____
— clothing	_____	_____	_____
— home repair center	_____	_____	_____
Near entertainment	_____	_____	_____
(list what kind)	_____	_____	_____
How far from work?	_____	_____	_____
(list miles or time)	_____	_____	_____
Horse property	_____	_____	_____
Close to neighbors	_____	_____	_____
(how close?)	_____	_____	_____
Far from neighbors	_____	_____	_____
(how far?)	_____	_____	_____
Near Fitness Club	_____	_____	_____
Near Park & Rec. area	_____	_____	_____
Near Community Center	_____	_____	_____
Has sewage hookup	_____	_____	_____
Has city water	_____	_____	_____
Has city gas	_____	_____	_____
Has city electric	_____	_____	_____
Paved Road to house	_____	_____	_____
Other	_____	_____	_____

Dream List

Neighborhood Checklist — Existing Homes

1. What does the home look like overall?

2. In what condition are the neighborhood homes?
   * outside yards, outside paint, parked cars, noise & activity level

3. What sort of noises do you hear?

4. What sort of smells do you smell?

5. What do you see when you look around?

6. How far are schools?

7. How do kids get to school?

8. Do you see graffiti & other signs of gang activity?

9. What are the PTA activities like?

10. Is there public transportation near?

11. Are there good, accessible roads near? What sort of shopping do you have nearby? How far?

12. Is it a safe neighborhood? (watch for bars on windows, gang activity, drug activity, etc.)

13. Are the adjacent neighborhoods consistent with this one? If not, what is the difference? (You do not want a nice neighborhood near a slummy one.)

Dream List

Neighborhood Checklist — New Homes

1. What is the builders' reputation (ask neighbors)?

2. Are new homes being constructed around you?

3. Are there amenities nearby?

4. What type of outside finishes and/or yard do you get if any?

5. What are your warranties?

6. Who is your contact person?

7. If something goes wrong in your home, how soon can you expect repair & help?

8. What sorts of other building is going on around you?

Dream List

Viewing Checklist — Inside

FLOORS

1. What are the floor coverings and what condition are they in:
   living room _____
   kitchen _____
   dining room _____
   hallways _____
   bathrooms _____
   dining room _____

2. Do the floors creak anywhere? _____

3. Are the floors even? _____

4. Are there broken tiles? _____

5. Is there any evidence of leakage in the bathrooms and/or kitchen? _____

PLUMBING

1. Are there leaking faucets? Check baths & kitchen _____

2. Secure sinks? _____

3. Turn water on to check for pressure _____

4. Leaky toilets? _____

5. Secure toilet bowl? _____

6. What condition are the fixtures in? _____

HEATING & COOLING UNITS

1. Ask how old are the units and what are the repairs made, if any. _____

_____

WATER HEATERS

1. What size is it? _____

2. Does it look rusty? _____

3. Are there signs of leakage? _____

Dream List

Viewing Checklist — Inside

GENERAL

1. What is the total square footage of livable space? _____

2. What are the rooms like?   Large enough?   Closet space?
   Windows?   Placement in house? _____

3. If there is a stairway, is it easy to use for your family? _____

4. Kitchen & Dining areas
   How does it feel to be in it? _____
   Do you like the cabinets? _____
   Do you like the counter space? _____
   Is there a pantry? _____
   Is the kitchen big enough? _____
   Look under the sink, any signs of leaks? _____
   Look in the cabinets, are the shelves straight or warped? _____
   What is the condition of the sink & fixtures. _____
   Does the garbage disposal work? _____
   Does the dishwasher work? _____
   Does the stove & range work? _____

WINDOWS & DOORS & SCREENS

1. Do the doors open easily?
   — Main entry _____
   — Bedrooms _____
   — Bathrooms _____
   — Closets _____
   — Sliding doors _____
   — Sliding screen doors _____

2. Do the windows open and close easily? _____
   — condition of window screens _____
   — condition of sliding door screens _____
   — condition of locks
      — doors _____
      — windows _____

Dream List

Viewing Checklist — Inside & Outside

LIGHTING & ELECTRICAL

1. Porch lights_____

2. Fixtures in
   - bedrooms _____
   - living room _____
   - dining room_____
   - kitchen _____
   - other _____

3. Are there plenty of outlets?_____

4. Do electrical outlets have enough amps to meet the needs of your
   appliances, computer, etc.? _____

GENERAL

1. Are there any bad smells?_____

2. Does the property drain adequately? _____

3. Where is sunrise & sunset? _____

4. Any particular noises? _____
   - machinery? _____
   - traffic? _____
   - heating, AC? _____
   - neighbors?_____

5. Lastly ask about insulation. What kind of insulation? _____
   Where is the insulation? _____

STORAGE

1. Size of garage _____
   - condition of garage _____

2. Washer/dryer area_____
   - utility sink_____

3. Basement size _____
   - basement condition_____
   - basement access_____

4. Is there an attic? Is it easy to get to? What condition is it in? _____
   - Is there a crawl space under the house? _____

Dream List

Viewing Checklist — Outside

1. As you approach the house, what is the road like?
   — easy access, unpaved, paved but bad, other _____

2. What does the outside of the house look like? _____

3. What is the condition of the roof? _____

4. What kind of landscaping? _____

5. What kinds of trees & shrubs? _____

6. If there is a pool, does it look in good condition? _____
   Are there cracks in it? _____
   Is it full of leaves and dirty? _____
   Are there a lot of trees around it? _____

7. Where does the electricity come from into the house? _____

8. What is the source of water _____

9. Is the house on septic? _____
   Sewer connected? _____
   Leach field? _____

10. What is the outside condition of the house:
    paint _____
    windows _____
    doors _____
    gates _____
    porches/enclosures _____
    fences _____
    patios _____
    faucets _____
    — where are they? _____
    — are they leaking? _____
    other structures _____

11. Heating & AC units — What condition are they in? _____

12. Steps — what condition are they in? _____

13. Driveway's condition _____

Dream List

Inspector Checklist

Here is a minimum number of things an inspector should check:

- Attic
- Basement
- Ceiling, walls, floors
- Door, windows, screens
- Foundation
- Electrical system
- Heating & cooling systems
- Insulation
- Ventilation
- Sewer lines
- Septic
- Wells
- Exterior Walls, decks, porches
- Property — drainage, fences, paved areas
- Garage
- Plumbing

The inspector is checking for the following:

1. Cracks & separation
2. Proper functioning of doors, windows, faucets, electrical outlets, etc.
3. Proper drainage of gutters
4. Proper drainage of sinks
5. Signs of leaks
6. Safety & proper electrical wiring
7. Condition of furnace & AC unit. If you live in hot climates, you may want a separate AC man to check the condition of the heating/cooling units.
8. Need for painting
9. Leakage in basement, attic, ceiling — look for water damage
10. Test to see the type & depth of insulation

Dream List

CLOSING COSTS

1. Deposit (earnest money) $ _____
2. Down payment   _____
3. Mortgage — monthly payment   _____
4. Loan application fee   _____
5. Points — total amount   _____
6. Loan origination fee   _____
7. Assumption fee   _____
8. Credit report fee   _____
9. Appraisal fee   _____
10. Home inspection (if you have one) _____
11. Processing fees   _____
12. Interest — prepaid   _____
13. Mortgage insurance   _____
14. Home insurance   _____
15. Property taxes   _____
16. Settlement fee   _____
17. Attorney fees   _____
18. Title search   _____
19. Title insurance   _____
20. Recording charge   _____
21. Transfer taxes   _____
22. Survey fees   _____
23. Homeowners' association fees   _____
24. Other   _____
25. Total closing costs $ _____

Dream List

PRE-CLOSING CHECKLIST

1. Final walk-through Date and time:_____

   — all things operational?_____

   — all items to be removed done? _____

   — all agreed on items in place? _____

2. Utilities

   — gas _____

   — electric_____

   — telephone _____

   — water _____

   — other services (garbage, etc.) _____

3. What documents do I need?_____

4. Total $ amount I need for closing_____

5. Time, place, date of closing _____

Dream List

CLOSING CHECKLIST

1. Hire an attorney, if necessary. _____

2. Make final financial arrangements. _____

3. Insure the mortgage, if appropriate. _____

4. Arrange for homeowners' insurance. _____

5. Get other needed insurance. _____

6. Have property surveyed and appraised. (If you go through a lending institution for a mortgage, it should handle these details.) _____

7. Arrange for general building inspection. _____

8. Arrange for specific inspections as needed. _____

   — roof _____

   — ac/heater _____

   — utilities _____

9. Arrange for termite inspection _____

10. Do final walk-through. _____

11. Ask about warranty deal. _____

12. Know your closing costs. _____

13. Have cashier's check prepared for closing. _____

14. Have the deed recorded after closing. _____

15. Other _____

Dream List

CLOSING COSTS CHECKLIST

Initial Mortgage Payment $ _____

Loan Origination Fee (charged by the lender)   _____

Loan Discount Fee (points charged by the lender)   _____

Loan Assumption Fee (if applicable)   _____

Prepaid Mortgage Insurance (if required)   _____

Credit Report cost   _____

Property Survey   _____

Inspections of Property cost   _____

Recording Deed   _____

Prepaid Homeowner's Insurance for First Year   _____

Prorated Property Taxes for Current Year   _____

Attorney's Fees   _____

Closing Company's Fees   _____

Title Search and Insurance (usually paid by seller)   _____

Credit Life Insurance   _____

Down Payment (earnest money)   _____

Balance Earnest Money Paid   _____

Other   _____

Total $ _____

Dream List

MOVING DAY CHECKLIST — PART I

1. Boxes — size & # needed: _____

_____

2. Mover's name: (or attach card)_____

Mover's address: _____

Mover's contact person & phone: _____

Estimated cost of moving: _____

3. If doing it yourself, Truck Co. Name: _____

address, tel #: _____

estimated cost of truck rental: _____

equipment needed: _____

blankets needed (for moving):_____

other items needed for packing the truck:_____

Total cost: _____

4. Who will help to move us?_____

_____

5. Time & place to meet:_____

6. Packing tape: (several rolls & min. 2 dispensers) _____

7. Marking pens (3 minimum):_____

8. When movers will arrive at new home: _____

9. Who will meet the movers: _____

10. What I need with me at the house first:_____

_____

11. What my children will need (food, toys, baby-sitter?):_____

_____

Dream List

MOVING CHECKLIST PART II

12. Change of address to post office: _____

13. Utilities

    gas: _____

    electric: _____

    water: _____

    garbage pickup: _____

    telephone: _____

14. Send "we've moved" cards to friends: _____

    (check off names in your telephone book as you send them)_____

15. Things I need to do to new home before I move:_____

    _____

    _____

    _____

    _____

16. Things I need to do to old home before I move:_____

    _____

    _____

    _____

    _____

17. Other: _____

    _____

    _____

    _____

Early in 1985, I bought an apartment complex with 20% down. I also purchased land under similar terms for an additional 150 units. By everyone's calculations, I made money when I bought, purchasing both at below their present value. At the time I bought the property real estate was used as a shelter against personal income. Because of that, it gave real estate a value beyond mere return on investment. Then came the Tax Reform Act of 1986 which disallowed depreciation, interest, and losses against personal income. Almost immediately, my properties were worth 40% less than I had paid. Since I had only 20% equity, I became what developers called, "upside down" in the properties.

We are now once again facing this problem from Washington. To pay partially for capital-gains breaks, Washington is trying to impose a new $250,000 maximum limit on the size of home mortgage that qualifies for interest deductions on IRS returns. This could be a huge blow for most Americans, especially those living in large urban areas.

Under current law, homeowners can deduct the interest paid on first mortgage balances up to $1 million.

If this change is enacted into law, it may create havoc. It will financially diminish the attractions of buying a home. It will be a blow to the entire housing industry which includes builders, tradespeople, the lumber industry, real estate agents, and the home decorating business. In a word, an entire infrastructure that depends on house building will suffer. So will you, the American home buyer.

The National Association of Realtors and the National Association of Home Builders did a study using $300,000 as the cap. They concluded that nationwide, 1.1 million taxpayers would have to pay higher taxes — by approximately $21 billion over the next five years. Using $250,000 as the cap would include a larger number of Americans and a larger tax amount.

A serious dent will also be put on resale prices of homes that are priced higher than $250,000. This can negatively affect a huge part of the American population.

Because of the diminished tax allowance, homes over $250,000 will be less desirable. This will drive prices down and cause a ripple effect on less expensive properties and drive their prices down as well. Homeowners will lose some or all of their equity. Some could become "upside down" as I had experienced.

Not only the rich suffer. Everyone suffers. The "ripple" effect will flow down to the least expensive homes. Every homeowner will lose. Tax incentives help give everyone the opportunity to have a home. This is what Americans want. We don't need less incentives; we need more.

My philosophy? Americans are entitled to and want a piece of the "American Dream." This is what America was built on. We should all work to keep and preserve it within our reach.

Call your congressmen; write to them; tell them how you feel about keeping your freedom and your rights.

For information and book orders, write or call:

Mike Domer Productions
7345 East Acoma, Suite 200
Scottsdale, AZ 85260
Tel: (602) 451-8000
Fax: (602) 451-8954